Behind
SEVEN
Locked Doors

By June Strandberg

Produced by:

FriesenPress
Suite 300 – 852 Fort Street
Victoria, BC, Canada V8W 1H8

www.friesenpress.com

Distributed to the trade by The Ingram Book Company

Acknowledgements

Sincere appreciation is extended to the following group of amazing people who helped to make both Beginnings and Just Beginnings a success. They believed in my dream that my plan would lead in the right direction to help marginalized women appreciate and value their lives, perhaps for the first time.

Beverly Roest, Program Director at the Burnaby Correctional Centre for Women, supported me every step of the way, loved what she did, and knew it mattered to every woman's life she touched. How fortunate for them that they crossed her path. She always listened to what they had to say and helped them with her wise words, letting them know she cared.

Beverly became the head of my Board of Directors when I started Just Beginnings in 2006. She was there to help make sure this special group of women knew our floral program offered something better for them in life. I so appreciated everything she did all those years. Thank you, Beverly.

John Pastorek, Head of Operations at the Burnaby Correctional Centre for Women, supported my program from day one. A very kind, gentle, understanding, and caring man, he was well respected in the prison by all the staff and inmates. He made sure every woman in BCCW was treated fairly and at all times kept safe. He made sure he knew each woman's situation, why they were incarcerated, what needed to be done to help improve their lives, and what it would take to accomplish this safely. He believed the floral program was a positive step and would offer a skill for the women while they were in prison, and that may be helpful to them upon their release. Thank you, John.

Michael and Ann Wilson of the Phoenix Society are two people that believed in my floral program and felt it would be a good partner in their new building that was to be the location of their new Education and Recovery Centre for Men with Addictions. Because my program was designed for recovering women, both our societies were working to achieve the same goals, pointing participants in the right direction for a better and clean life They were always there with full support and wise words of encouragement. They both devoted so much to making a difference in so many people's lives, and they were there to make sure my dream of Just Beginnings really did happen. So it was, in February, 2006, that we unlocked our doors, opened our little coffee counter, full service flower shop, and a fully equipped School of Floral Design We were ready to start. To those two special people that helped make it all possible, thank you, Michael and Ann.

Marlene Yakabuski, our devoted bookkeeper, worked tirelessly in our office handling all the business for the flower shop and the school. Always looking on the brighter side, she was the glue that helped keep us together when we were in doubt. She put in so very many long hours to make sure everything was done correctly and on time. Thank you, Marlene, you were so valuable to us and we treasured your friendship.

To my daughter-in-law Liz, thank you for your creative ideas on the photography for the front cover of my book.

Georgia Nieken contributed so many hours serving on my Board of Directors, and always supported and helped me so much in every way that she could. At times, when things looked impossible, Georgia was always there to restore my hope. She helped give birth to my ideas and she was never without an encouraging word.

To my very positive sister, always there to cover my back, thank you, Georgia.

My niece, Michele Bond volunteered many hours at Just Beginnings, not only in the office but by assisted me in our floral design classes, helping students with their floral projects. She also contributed many hours during the 2010 Olympics with the packing and shipping of the Olympic victory bouquets. Thank you, Michelle.

Jack Roest, Beverly's husband, spent endless hours devoted to our floral school. He connected with the organizations that were involved with marginalized women, helping to choose the ones that could benefit the most from our floral course and representing us at meetings and workshops. He always made sure all the repairs were done in the school, and that it was clean and very organized. Jack was always kind, pleasant, considerate, and contributed a great deal to Just Beginnings. Thank you, Jack.

To all my Board of Directors, for all the endless hours that they volunteered and contributed to making sure Just Beginnings was always on the right track, both in the flower shop and our floral design school. Thank you very much.

Margitta Schulz, being such a big part of the 2010 Winter Olympics was awesome. It was a special honor being able to have my floral students from Just Beginnings proudly arrange the 1,800 Olympic victory bouquets. The added bonus was to partner with Margitta and to bond a friendship that will last forever. I cherish the connections, the relationships, and the memories that we can treasure for many years to come. Thank you, Margitta.

To all the women behind those "Seven Locked Doors" that helped make Beginnings flower shop one of the best in the Vancouver lower mainland. To all the dedication and pride they put into every arrangement they made, no matter whether it was for the bride, the graduate, a birthday or an anniversary, the arrival of a new baby, or the loss of someone dear. The magic of those beautiful flowers helped to heal each and every one of them.

Dedicated to my three children.

Casey, who spent fourteen years with me at the Burnaby Correctional Centre for Women, working side by side with me and every inmate staff that we had, teaching them to be the best florists they could be. She always set a great example.

Cindy, who always supported what I was doing in that prison, and was always there for me. I am so grateful and proud to have her as my daughter.

Dean, who at a very young age told me he would always take care of me and to never worry. He even mentioned that he would pay all my bills forever. He has always been there for me with his wise words. What else could a mother want?

Having their loving presence in my life is a special gift. What a lucky woman I am to have three such wonderful kids. I'm so very proud of them.

With all my love to my grandchildren: Quintan, Kelsea, Dean, Mathew, Spencer, and my great grandson Wyatt, as well as my two wonderful son-in-laws, Dan Morley and Gord Lawton.

Introduction

In a little corner of my heart I keep a place for my dreams to dwell.

I had a dream, a vision to develop a program for women incarcerated in prison that would train them to be floral designers. During the training each woman would also learn valuable life lessons such as cultivating a willingness to learn, a determination to be the best, and to motivate appreciation for respect in herself and in others. The program would plant the seed of honesty along with dependability, responsibility, and, as confidence grew, so would each woman gain much needed self-esteem. My dream was also to help participants not to worry about what they were, but to look at what they could be by overcoming obstacles that seemed insurmountable, and then focus on achieving goals.

Our program motto was:

Live your life from your heart and share your sadness with someone you love.

For today and all your tomorrows, count your blessings, and turn your attitude into gratitude.

In 1990 I presented my proposal to the decision makers at the prison site. After a detailed review it was accepted and the floristry program was born. It was the only one of its kind in Canada and received worldwide attention. Representatives from institutions in Canada, the USA, and Scotland came to see how this unique program worked.

BEAUTY (1996)

People say beauty is in the eye of the beholder
When you are suddenly taken away from the
real world and transported somewhere very
unreal,

Things of beauty are a rare thing to find.
After you have adjusted to the pale bleakness
around,

You think you are immune, but truly you are not.
Then suddenly something of beauty comes
shining through.

I think of this and realize
That one little thing of beauty was that fragrant little flower

I would like to acknowledge all the poetry and words I have included in my book that represent the work from the inmates at the Burnaby Correctional Centre for Women, who took part in the school's writing sessions.

The poems are from the fifth edition of *Words From Within* and are used with permission after consultation with British Columbia Corrections.

Chapter One

My long journey began over sixty two years ago and was a pathway that took me in so many directions. Like any path you might take, it was sometimes smooth other times rocky, sometimes sunny and warm, and maybe stormy with heavy clouds. Never knowing what might be around the next turn, I wondered if I could handle what was in store for my future, however early on in my life, I knew where I stood was my own private space and it was up to me to decide who I let into that space.

My life as a little girl was lonely and sad. I was five years old when World War II began in September, 1939, and my father went away to serve Canada in the Royal Canadian Navy. Not only my father joined the services but so did two of my uncles. Times were very difficult during the war years; food was severely rationed with government issued coupons required to buy meat, sugar, coffee, tea, and many other groceries.

The war changed my Dad. When he came home he had a difficult time finding work, and he and my mother seemed to drink more than I ever remembered. When I was eight years old my sister Diane was born and I became responsible for looking after her and my cousin Barb, who was three years younger than me.

By the time I was ten years old we were left alone so often, never knowing what we might have to eat. But time went by and as I grew older I knew I had to look after myself. My parents were alcoholics and had very little time for their children.

It is now when I look back at my life as a lonely, sad, neglected little girl this experience led me to make choices. At that time there was no one there to be supportive or see me through the rough patches. So many things could have influenced me to go down the wrong path. We are all born good, but over time I came to see how easy it is to make a poor decision. This can be the one that leads us down that rocky road that can change our life forever.

At sixteen years old I graduated from high school but I had no idea what I wanted to do. Our family home was in Calgary, Alberta, and my dad was a chef on the dining cars of the Canadian Pacific Railway. He got me my first job to train as a Morse code operator with the CPR for $300.00 per month, which in 1950 was very good pay. The job required me to work a split shift from 8 am to 12 noon, and again from 3 pm to 7 pm. Rather than go all the way home, I would spend those in between hours at my Uncle Tommy's flower shop, James Morris Florist, just a few blocks from the railway station.

It was not long before my uncle started teaching me all about working with beautiful flowers and I loved every minute of it. He was a wonderful teacher and a beautiful floral designer. He taught me to make a bridal bouquet in the cascade style, which is a lovely work of art. I completed my first funeral casket spray with gladiolus and roses and accompanied my Uncle Tom to deliver it to the Jaques Funeral Home just before prayers for the deceased would be offered that evening. I waited in the office with the manager while my uncle went into the chapel to place the spray on the coffin. He returned quickly and said, "June, the flower spray is too short." Luckily he was prepared and had brought six extra gladiolus with him in case there was some breakage during the delivery. Uncle Tom told me to take those flowers and fix the problem so that the flowers covered the casket properly. I knew without asking that there was a person already in that casket, and I said I thought he could do the repair much quicker than I, but his answer to my suggestion was, "You made it, you fix it." The only thing I did not know was that the top half of the casket was open and I could see the dear lady lying there peacefully. I was terrified but, knowing that mourners were going to arrive in a few minutes, I hurriedly started to place three of the long-stemmed flowers at the bottom end of the arrangement. It was very difficult to insert the extra flowers at the top of the arrangement since I had to place the long-stemmed flowers over the lady's face to get them into the correct position. Luckily I managed to fix my mistake without disturbing a hair on her head. I got out of that funeral room as fast as I could.

Flowers made me realize what I valued most, which was the opportunity every day to work with something so profoundly beautiful. That was the day I became aware of the talent that was within me, what I had, and all I was meant to be. The day came when my uncle said to me, "June, you can't be a Morse code operator. You need to be a florist. Tell your dad you want to leave your job and come to work for me." My uncle told me my wage would start at $14.27 per week.

I went home that night knowing I had to tell my dad what I intended to do. In the morning, as my dad lay in bed reading the newspaper, I could see that he had a hangover and was not in a good mood. I sat on the edge of the bed and, choosing my words very carefully, I said, "Dad I want to quit the CPR."

He looked up at me with a very angry expression and said, "What the hell are you talking about? What do you want to do?"

I answered without hesitation. "I'm going to be a florist with Uncle Tommy."

His reply was, "Are you crazy, you would give up your good job at the CPR as a Morse code operator to be a florist?" He paused and looked me squarely in the eyes and said very sternly, "If you're going to do this you'd better be the best damn florist that ever was. Do you hear me?"

"Yes dad, I will be. I promise you."

My Uncle Tom was that special person who inspired me to be a florist and to love flowers the way he did. He believed in me, shared his knowledge and passion, and made me realize I could be the very best florist.

I knew I needed to share that talent and love of flowers with those individuals that could use this perfect gift for a better and happier life. It would be my personal choice to make sure this happened and to know I was moving in the right direction. Over the years, as I grew into an award winning florist and the owner of two flower shops and a trade school, I kept my promise to my dad. I think he would have been proud of my efforts.

My mother always supported my decision and often was there to help me in my flower shops. She was not a designer, but she loved to sell flowers, and was always a great help.

It was not long before I came to another turn on my path. James Morris Florist was located on 7th Avenue in downtown Calgary. My close friend Kay worked at an automotive company on 6th Avenue, and we would meet most days for lunch. One day she mentioned there was a brake mechanic working in the company who wanted my phone number. Apparently he had passed us on the street a few days previously when we were on our lunch break. She ran over one day on her coffee break, came in the back door of the flower shop, and asked me if I could talk to her for a minute. She said with such excitement, "June, Allan wants to ask you out on a date!" I let her give him my number, however I turned him down a few times before I finally weakened and we met. Allan came to pick me up in his old Ford convertible that had a little rumble seat in the back, but lacked fenders on the back wheels. This small detail caused me some worry as he started to drive down my street that was very wet and muddy due to melting snow. I was wearing my brand new winter coat that quickly became splashed with mud. My hair also suffered the same fate, however none of this seemed to bother Allan; he was taking his girl to a show. So began my first memorable date with him.

Allan's next car was almost as bad. I had to place my feet on either side of a big hole in the floor, and if we drove through a big puddle, the water would splash up on me. He finally put a piece of wood over the hole, but he thought if it was open and the brakes failed, I could drag my feet. If the car didn't start right away maybe I could use my feet to get us going, who knows! I fell in love with Allan Marchand, who was to become my first husband. Coincidently, his father was also a chef on the private cars with the CPR and he knew my dad.

Our journey together was sometimes smooth and happy with lots of love, and at times sad like a rough, bumpy road. In the early part of dating we decided to call it quits and I was heartbroken. My mother and dad decided to send me by train to Boston, Massachusetts, to stay with my Aunt Hazel and Uncle Bob. I left my job at James Morris Florist and travelled east to Boston, staying there for two years working full time in a flower shop and part time in a five and dime store in Malden, a short distance from Boston.

I wasn't there very long when Allan telephoned and asked me to come home, so I returned to Calgary. We married in 1955, and in 1957 I gave birth to our son Dean. We moved to Boston where Allan received more training in air controls, returning to Canada shortly after Dean's second birthday. In 1960 we were blessed with our baby girl Cindy.

Over the next few years my mother and dad decided to move to Vancouver B.C., where my dad's brother lived, taking my younger sisters Georgia and Penny with them. I missed my mother, and Dean and Cindy missed both of their grandparents. I still had my sister Diane in Calgary but in a short time her marriage ended and she also moved to Vancouver.

During my years with Allan I returned to work for my uncle. However, by the time Cindy was three years old and Dean was six, our marriage had started to fall apart. In 1964 I decided to leave Allan. I packed a few things and, along with my children, moved to Vancouver to be with my parents. It was only ten days later that Allan left his good job, packed up all our furniture, and followed us. He had a great work reputation and very quickly had another good job and we were together again as a family.

I was able to get a job with Grace McCarthy at Flowers by Grayce. She was a great lady and this was to be another step in my floral career. I managed Grace's shop at the Bayshore Inn and was fortunate to meet some special celebrities. Johnny Mathis stopped in more than once for flowers. He was a very handsome, well-spoken gentleman and was staying at the hotel while he was performing in Vancouver. I also looked after Flowers by Grayce in the Hotel Vancouver for a short time. We had a large artificial dogwood tree, the provincial flower of British Columbia, in the centre of the flower shop. The trunk of the tree was real and the flowers were artificial, but it looked like a dogwood tree had been planted in the shop.

I was surprised one quiet afternoon when a gentleman walked into the flower shop, circled the tree, and asked me "Is this a real tree?" I was speechless for a few seconds as I realized the voice belonged to Bob Hope. He wanted a red carnation boutonniere because he was being photographed in the hotel by Yousuf Karsh, one of the most famous and accomplished portrait photographers of all time. I made the boutonniere and pinned it on Mr. Hope with great pleasure!

While I was at Flowers by Grayce my good friend John Ledgerwood, manager of Woodward's Stores flower department, asked me if I would like to come and work there. He needed another designer, the wages were good, and I liked teaming with John as he was a beautiful designer and we had won awards together years before. So off to Woodward's I went. It was a very busy flower department, but there were times when business would slow down and my hours were shortened. One day I was in the staff lunch room and noticed a sign announcing that Woodward's were building a new store in Surrey and, including their other four stores, they needed to increase their number of store detectives from four women to six. I thought I could work part time in the flower department and, if Woodward's trained me, I could work some of my time as a store detective. The job was mine. I was thoroughly trained and partnered with Mary Bailey, but returned to work in the floral department during busy seasons.

My experiences as a store detective were much more than I ever expected. On my first day on the floor I was in the meat department when a young man decided to steal four steaks. I saw him hide them inside his heavy overcoat. As he left the store I followed him through the door, slipped my arm through his and told him he had merchandise that he had neglected to pay for. He did not come easily and in our struggle he pulled the sleeve off my raincoat, however, I managed to get him to the freight elevator and upstairs to security.

We had been trained not to go outside the store with a shop-lifter. We were to apprehend them when they would go through the first exit doors and before they went out the second set of doors to the street, but this did not always work. Some shoplifters would grocery shop with a cart, pushing it out to their car without paying. In that case we would call for back up, both of us following the thief outside.

Once there was an elderly lady who stole two tins of salmon. I hated to pick her up because she looked so destitute, but it was my job, I had to do it. The man that took the electric saw from the hardware department said when I took him that he wasn't stealing it, he just wanted to take it outside to show his friend that was waiting for him in the car.

One time a Russian freighter had docked in Vancouver to load water and supplies. Two women from the ship had been sent to our grocery department, and I noticed them as soon as they came in because they were very large and tall. I thought it a good idea to keep an eye on them as they quickly filled four shopping bags with food. They pushed their grocery cart over to the exit doors, removed the shopping bags, and began to leave the store. My partner and I apprehended them before they exited but we were really no match for them. When we got a hold on them they threw the bags, spilling groceries everywhere. Finally we managed to escort the women upstairs where our security manager contacted the ship, summoning the captain and the first officer to the store. The next morning the Vancouver Sun newspaper told the story and to our amazement the thieves were let go. The ship left port with no charges being laid. The newspaper noted that similar shoplifting had happened in other ports.

The stories were many over my time as a store detective, but I always enjoyed returning to the flower department when I was needed. I think I was the only florist store detective in town! Over that period I saw another dark side of life and heard the sad stories behind each of the shoplifters. Spending time being a store detective was another stepping stone that made me see how lost and sad people's lives can be, however this does not make shop lifting or breaking the law an acceptable way for them to meet their insurmountable needs. Most of the shoplifters I dealt with were broken and so desperate, selling what they stole to have money for another drug fix, food for themselves or their children, alcohol, or simply a roof over their head. The demands that were put on them by the pressures from the life they were living at the time, the many times they were pushed aside and forgotten, or made to feel worthless, I remember the experience of how I felt at that time, even though they had done wrong, deep inside me I wished I could help them out of that life. It was like no one cared, just charge them, put them in jail and throw away the key. They committed a crime they deserve to do the time. The deep wounds inside them cannot always be fixed by sending them to jail.

I learned there were many different kinds of shoplifters all breaking the law for different reasons. The ones that are part of a crime ring are part of something much bigger, not like the scared, timid lady who stole a box of Kraft Dinner and two tins of cat food.

Over the next four years Allan and I tried hard to keep our marriage together, but it wasn't meant to be. Our life together as we knew it came to an end in 1968, one week before Christmas. As I arrived home with Dean and Cindy I knew something was wrong. There was a Christmas tree in our living room, but it had always been our tradition to pick out a special tree together as a family. My heart sank and I knew at that moment that Allan was gone. I sat down at the kitchen table, opened the letter he had left for me, and began to cry. Dean and Cindy ran to me, and Dean sat down in his dad's place at the table. They knew he had left us. Dean placed his hand on mine and said, "Please don't cry, Mom. I will always take care of you, and I will pay all the bills for you." I will remember that moment and those tender words forever. From that day forward I knew it would not be easy but, although we were falling apart, the love the three of us had for each other would hold us together. I knew I had to have the courage to overcome the challenges ahead of me. Allan had met someone and I agreed to a divorce. He was the love of my life, and that love will remain in the corner of my heart always. First loves are never over. On the day our divorce petition was to be held at the Vancouver Court House we stopped to have a coffee at the Hotel Georgia. As we sat there Allan said, "Let's stop this before it's too late. We don't have to go through with this." But the hand had already been dealt and our divorce was granted that day. We had thirteen years together and I wouldn't trade one year of that time of my life. I was thankful for my two beautiful children, what a big part of my life they were, and how much happiness they brought into my life every day. It was hard for Dean and Cindy not to have their dad in their everyday lives.

Life's challenges help make you what and who you are. If you stop feeling sad for a moment you will see life is worthwhile and you just keep trying.

Allan remarried and the kids would see him from time to time. We managed on our own but missed him. I dated but compared each man to Allan. No one could fill his shoes at that time, however the day came when that door started to close and a new door opened.

Dad played a part in my life once more. He had a very good friend, Casey DeMetz, who had worked at the Canadian Pacific Railway as a train man and was now retired. He told my dad that his only son Bob was retiring from a long career with the Canadian Air Force and he and his wife were moving from Ontario to settle in British Columbia.

A big welcome home party was held at the local Legion, to which my mom and dad were invited. They thought it would be nice for me to go with them and it was there that I was introduced to Bob DeMetz. While we danced we talked and I mentioned I had two children, while he had none. Before the evening ended Bob mentioned that his wife would leave the following day to visit her mother in Squamish for one week and that he would like to take Dean, Cindy, and me to Stanley Park. It was Sunday and I thought it would be a nice change for the children. We had a wonderful day. During that week Bob visited often and on the last night he asked me to go out to dinner with him, but deep inside me I knew this wasn't quite the thing to be doing. Bob explained that he and his wife wanted to end their marriage before coming to Vancouver. He was a very special man and I enjoyed being with him. At the end of the evening, as we sat talking in his car, he kissed me and surprised me saying, "June, I have fallen in love with you." I felt the same way and was happy that I would not be the cause of breaking his marriage. I never thought I could find another man I would love like Allan, but there he was sitting beside me one week after meeting him.

Bob and I started to spend all our time together and within the year we decided to marry. It was 1969. We had a lovely wedding with close friends and family around us. The following year we had a sweet baby girl that we named Casey after Bob's dad, who sadly died just before we married, never meeting his little granddaughter.

Several years before I met Bob I left my job at Flowers by Grayce and went to work for Flowers by Elizabeth. When I became pregnant I left Elizabeth's, taking a year off. My mother again babysat Dean, Cindy, and Casey when I returned to work, and this time I freelanced at a number of flower shops, working with some of the best designers in Vancouver. In 1973 I started designing for several floral wholesale companies. This was a wonderful experience, being able to work in teams with designers from Canada and the United States. I travelled across Canada and the west coast of the United States competing in floral design shows and winning several awards.

Dean graduated from high school in 1975 and went to work for his dad in air controls. Cindy graduated three years later and entered college to study as a dental assistant, but in 1979 became a flight attendant with Canadian Pacific Airlines. For a very long time I wanted to have my own flower shop and with Dean's help I realized my dream, opening The Bayside School of Floral Design and Bayside Flower Shop in 1982. This dream was also to change my daughter Casey's life. She was an excellent student, but while in grade nine she began to miss classes and was in danger of being expelled from school. I decided to immediately take her out of school and brought her to my floral school. While she completed her high school through correspondence courses she also helped out in the office, the design school, and the flower shop. Casey's career as a florist had started.

My husband Bob was my best support and always a great help. He delivered our flower orders, kept our books balanced, and maintained the store. He even learned to clean flowers properly. Since I have never driven a car, Bob drove me to the flower auction twice a week and most days made sure that Casey got to school. I couldn't have made it in any of our flower shops without him. He believed in me and always had comforting words during the rough patches, forever sharing his love with Dean, Cindy, Casey, and me. Bob was a very special person in my life.

Chapter Two

Little did I know that my flower shop and floral design school venture was to dramatically change my life. One afternoon, not long after opening the school, I received a call from a social service officer asking if I would train two prison parolees in my school. I accepted their offer and two young women arrived to start the six week course. By the end of their first week I noticed little interest or participation from these two new students, who also did not mix with the other students. I contacted the office and advised them that the training was not working out. The ministry contact asked me if I would give them one more week as the students were very nervous, had never been in a class room setting, and mixing with strangers was very difficult for them. Talking with them in my no nonsense style, they soon understood what I was trying to say to them and both women, who were very artistic, passed the practical and theory course work with flying colors. I was able to place one in a major department store flower shop in downtown Vancouver, where she later became the manager. The other went to work for a friend of mine on Vancouver Island and, after working there for many years, bought the shop from my friend when she retired. I stayed in touch with these women for many years. The feeling I had from helping the two parolees never left me. I saw firsthand what flowers could do to help heal a broken life. Over the next several years in our school we turned out a number of excellent florists. Some started their own businesses and others went to work throughout British Columbia.

Every day I witnessed what working with flowers could do to your life. My own broken alcoholic life needed mending. There was a void deep inside me and I was using alcohol to fill it. I realized some time after I stopped drinking that I had not really acknowledged I was an alcoholic and so it began again.

In 1979 I joined Alcoholics Anonymous for the first time. I was very good at hiding my addiction and tried my best not to let it interfere with my work, but it was starting to affect my health. I didn't quite make it to my first year and started my bad habit once again. By the time I was preparing to start The Bayside School of Floral Design and Flower Shop I knew I had to put a cork in that bottle again or life as I knew it would be over. It had been three years since I first joined AA and dropped out, so that guilty feeling was with me all that time. I felt I had let myself down. One night Bob had gone to bed and I stayed up to drink alone. There was an unopened forty ounce bottle of vodka in the kitchen and I went to pour another drink. At that moment something stopped me, or as the AA program calls it, a miracle happened. I took that bottle and poured it down the sink and from that night in 1982, alcohol has never passed my lips. That's the night my life took a dramatic change. The light came on and I was finally in control. I could have, do, or accomplish anything I wanted. All my dreams could come true. That is when I realized there was something more powerful out there than I ever realized. I knew I was opening new avenues and with every breath, every thought, and every step I took I would never be alone again. No matter how rocky the road might be, how bad the storm, or when sadness comes my way, there is a presence with me and it's steady, strong, and full of love. It will forever be there to help me climb the highest mountain and I will always get to the other side. At the end of that rainy day there will always be a rainbow and for sure that pot of gold. I am so very grateful. Life is good.

Looking after the school and the flower shop was hard work, but the rewards were the bonus for the long hours. In 1985 one of the large floral wholesale companies offered me a position as a design consultant, offering excellent salary and a great opportunity. I talked it over with Bob who, in the previous year, had been diagnosed with mouth cancer, making me consider selling the flower shop and closing my trade school. I did this after a number of months without any regrets, believing that letting go of one dream would allow me to achieve other goals. I was also concerned about Bob's health and together we had to believe that he would beat his cancer. He did believe and always did his best to be positive. So many times he would say to me, "June I'm going to make it, don't worry, I'll be around for a long time, kid."

I started the job with the floral wholesale company in 1986, travelling back and forth across Canada, designing and showing florists the product and the many ways to design with it. Some would consider this to be a dream job and I enjoyed my time there, but I still felt there had to be something better for me. I had a lot of knowledge and wanted to teach people about flowers and designing, not to florists who already know about the trade.

My thoughts returned to those two young women who had been paroled from prison and attended my floral design school. I thought about how those beautiful flowers had changed their lives. Their experiences touched my life, letting me realize there's nothing as real as a dream. Knowing that every day I open my eyes, I'm capable of making it another absolutely wonderful day, not only for me but also for others, and having a few flowers in my hands could help make it so.

One day in the summer of 1989 it occurred to me that a prison for women would be the place to take my dream to change lives through flowers, but I didn't even know if there was a prison for females in British Columbia. Undaunted by the fact that I had absolutely no experience in the world of corrections, but knowing that I wanted to work with female inmates, I telephoned the Oakalla prison in the city of Burnaby and discovered that women prisoners were housed there in a section called Lakeside. That afternoon I arrived at Oakalla to meet with Beverly Roest, the program director for the soon to be opened Burnaby Correctional Centre for Women. The prison was nearly empty of inmates because the men had already been moved to their new location, but the women were still at Lakeside. I met Beverly and presented my idea to put a flower shop and training centre in the prison. Beverly said, "We are not going to be here, however your timing is perfect, we are building a new facility." She asked me if I had anything on paper and I said, yes. She wanted me to bring all the information back to her in a couple of days. That night I spent at the computer with my neighbour's son Brett, who was going to university at the time and knew exactly how to prepare a presentation for my program. Two days later I returned to Lakeside and proudly placed my plan in front of Beverly. She reviewed it carefully, saying, "This is unbelievable. As far as I'm concerned this is a go." At that time initial program acceptance was by a handshake endorsement, with a full proposal containing financial data prepared for the provincial attorney-general.

I returned to work that day and gave one month's notice to Rick, who had hired me three years before. He was surprised that I was leaving my good job and asked about my plans. He was speechless when I told him that I was going into the women's new prison to teach inmates to be florists. I think he thought I had lost my mind, but I assured him confidently that this was something I really wanted to do and knew it was the right decision.

Chapter Three

Within days Beverly asked me to come back to Lakeside, bring some flowers, and talk with the inmates about the program.

She met me and led me through several locked doors and dreary corridors in the old prison. As we made our way through I detected a terrible musty odor and suddenly had a nervous feeling in the pit of my stomach. For a brief moment I wondered if I had made the right decision, but when I finally walked through the doors of the gymnasium and could see a group of twelve inmates seated around a table, I knew that what I was going to do there was right. As I looked at the women I had expected something entirely different, thinking they would be rough and coarse and wearing striped prison clothes. This was not the case. They were all quite tidy looking in their uniform grey sweats. Beverly introduced me and explained briefly why I was there. The inmates sat quietly while I outlined what my program was all about. Before I arrived I had pre-cut flowers and prepared containers ready for their use. To my surprise, as well as the twelve women sitting around the table ready to start, there were about fifteen more women inmates standing around the table as onlookers, curious as to what was going to take place. Also present was Sarah McEwen, the future director of minimum security in the new prison, and two guards.

I divided the flowers evenly, showing how to place them in the container correctly. I was the only one with a pair of scissors in case something needed cutting. We started our arrangements and the inmates took direction very well. They did a surprisingly good job. However, there was one inmate who looked as if she had just stepped out of a shower. Her long hair was wet and dripping down her shoulders. Her t-shirt was wet too so I knew she had jumped into those clothes right out of her shower. But it was not just her appearance; each flower she picked up from her little bundle of cut flowers she thought needed to be shorter. Rather than give them to me to cut with my scissors she chewed the end off with her teeth, and didn't always spit out the leftover stem. This bothered me and I offered to cut them for her but she liked doing it her way.

The women completed their arrangements and I was amazed to see how well each one had done. I received approval earlier that allowed the inmates to keep their arrangements. As they were getting ready to leave I told them what a good job they had done and they were to take that arrangement back to their cells with them. One of the girls stood up and said, "Will you come back?"

Without hesitation my answer was loud and clear. "Yes, I will, and I'll make a florist out of anyone that would like to try." I received a big round of applause from everyone in the room. That was also my first experience getting a lot of big hugs from a group of women in jail. Each hug went straight to my heart and I knew then that my flowers and I were going to make a difference in these women's lives.

My thoughts went back to the day my Uncle Tom said, "June, you need to be a florist." I knew without a doubt these beautiful flowers had to be in my life, and from that day forward I have been one of the luckiest people in the world. I get to touch, hold, smell, and look at one of nature's most beautiful commodities every day. To know that these flowers would be going to someone else who needed to have them to make their day better, to put a smile on their face, to ease any pain and sorrow that they might be experiencing, or even to let them know someone loved them enough to give them these beautiful little gems.

I also realized that day that flowers are often taken for granted and overlooked for the impact they make. From weddings, to funerals, the sick bed, first day on the job, a happy birthday, the "sorry I missed our anniversary", "congratulations on the new baby", and on and on, they are the only personalized item you can have arranged beautifully and delivered to someone special half way around the world in eight hours' time, letting them know that you are thinking of them and love them. What better way to say it but with flowers.

In 1991 the Burnaby Correctional Centre for Women (BCCW) opened with both a secure custody unit and an open living unit. A joint federal and provincial project, the centre was designed to house all women remanded to custody or sentenced in British Columbia. While incarcerated the women received support in areas such as training for future employment, personal growth, or with various interests they may have.

Prior to inmates arriving at the new facility all instructors were required to present their programs to various stakeholders connected to the prison; programs such as Tailoring, Hair and Beauty, Horticulture and Flowers, Cooking. At this point only Beverly Roest, and the Head of Prison Operations, John Pastorek, believed in my vision and I knew I would be challenged. I presented to judges and lawyers, followed by guards, staff security, the prison warden, and anyone else who needed to know how institutional programs worked. I gave them packages that contained full information on how I planned to make my program successful including all costs and supplies that would be required. The tools were a big stumbling block. Knives, scissors, wire cutters, bolt cutters, secateurs, and rose strippers in a prison program? They all said it could not happen. I could not have those tools around inmates.

Then my question was Do the inmates have knives and forks to eat with? Would they have scissors in the beauty parlour and the tailor shop? How did they cut the material? How would the horticulture program handle all the tools they needed? The answers to those questions were all yes, and I received their consent to have all my tools. Three large shadow boxes were made to contain the tools of the trade, two for the design room and one in my office. The boxes had outlines of each tool we used and we were given safety instructions to follow. The boxes were unlocked at the start of each day. Inmates were required to sign the tools out and again when they returned them. Casey and I also had to sign after each name, every time. During the day we were to survey the room regularly to make sure the tools were at each bench with every inmate, and it was imperative that every tool was counted and signed off before any inmate was allowed to leave the room. If for any reason we could not account for one knife, scissors, or any of the tools, we had to report this to prison control immediately. Our door would be locked at all times, but if a tool went missing, no one could leave the room or gain entry until it was found. Most often if an inmate lost a tool it had fallen into the garbage with the flower clippings. We always found them, but there was an incident during our time there when the prison was on a complete lock down for three days, meaning every square inch of that prison was searched. The missing tool was finally found; we went through all the flower shop trash bags once more and had overlooked it. I was aware before I went into the prison that knives can disappear, it happens in flower shops too, and I knew I would have to be extra cautious.

During the year before the prison opened I experienced many negative responses to my program. The idea of a floral training class was bizarre. Some of the guards thought putting wire cutters, scissors, and rose strippers into prisoners' hands would make their job much harder. From the start there were challenges and barriers but I believed I could succeed. No one had ever seen or heard of a floral program in a maximum security prison. 'Beginnings' would be the only florist training program and flower shop behind bars in North America, or anywhere in the world as far as we researched. One of my first requests was that no guards be present in my area. There were no cameras in our flower shop or in the training centre. Even though Casey and I were supposed to wear a personal security alarm, we never did as we did not feel our safety was ever in jeopardy. It was important to me to treat the women the way I would want to be treated myself, despite the fact that I knew I would be working with inmates that would have committed multiple murders, robbery, fraud, and many other crimes, that they would be drug addicts or suffer from many dangerous illnesses. Safety was not an issue; we were all women and I was not interested in what they had done, what they had been, or what they were. I just knew they were broken women. Many had lost their families, kids, and self-respect.

My beautiful flowers were going to relieve some of the pain and help restore some hope; they did not have to be lost or forgotten anymore. These inmates had been hardened by years of abuse and many had spent time in institutions from a young age. Their lives are filled with sadness, disappointment, loss, no love or praise, and no appreciation for who they were. Some of this terrible treatment started when they were little children. They were physically, mentally, and sexually abused then cast away to make it in life as best they could. Any attention or sign of love they might have received over these many years they took to help fill that big hole in their hearts. More often than not that attention came from the wrong place and there was a very dear price to pay for it. They almost sold their souls and when you looked in their eyes there was never a twinkle, just blank looks full of fear and sadness. My instinct took over and I knew right away I wanted to put something beautiful into their lives, something that when you looked at it and smelled the lovely fragrance it would put a little warm spot inside and a little twinkle would come into your eye. It was like taking a magic pill. These beautiful flowers were going to help heal each one of them. I absolutely knew this to be true.

When the new prison was opened and my program was to begin, I came through the front door and was told by control to sign the book. I was then given an identity tag to wear and handed my key card that would open every door between the outside world and my flower shop.

An Untitled Poem

So who are they to pass
judgement on me?
If only they had time
to look and see.

Just throw me away because
I am bad,
But deep down inside
I am just sad.

If only they had time
I would tell them why I did the crime.
It's not for a dime and it's not for the drugs
I guess I'm lacking, for a better term, hugs.

Attention it might be
I am yet to see.
Was it really me?
Who am I?

★★★★

An Untitled Poem

As I sit under lock and key
I think they've been unfair to me.
For here I sit and do my time
Being a junkie my only crime.

It would be better to rehabilitate
Than to fill us full of grudge and hate.
For I have put no-one in any harm
To stick a needle in my arm.

Chapter Four

Here I was all alone behind seven locked doors, but I was ready, knowing the resident students would be arriving within the half hour. I had been given a list with the names of eight women that would be attending my first class, and had been briefed on the history of each participant. My students were Suzy, Anita, Marilyn, Dina, Elaine, Crystal, Linnet, and Maryanne. Anita was an older lady who was incarcerated on a murder charge. She was very withdrawn and sad, stayed in her cell, and never mixed with the others. She was unlike the other inmates, being close to my age and had lived a respectful life, always worked hard, had a good job, raised her family, and was known to be a very nice person. Something very tragic happened to Anita that pushed her to the very edge. After a long trial she was given a life sentence of twenty five years with the provision to apply for parole after serving ten. I read all the names on my list and knew I had been following her murder trial in the newspaper all these months.

When my students walked through the door I asked them to find a place at a design bench. I introduced myself and asked them their names. Without Anita saying her name I knew who she was.

Her eyes were focused down, her shoulders were slumped over, and her whole appearance was one of sadness and despair.

All of a sudden when I looked at them and saw what a group of lost, broken women really looked like, my heart sank. A feeling of overwhelming sadness came over me. I got a lump in my throat and it was all I could do not to let tears come into my eyes.

I knew the very first day in that prison I could never let any doubt enter into my mind about what I was here to do. That day marked my life for all the years to come.

I knew that every one of these women was going to be, and have, something they had never experienced when I was finished with them. That was self-confidence, pride, self-esteem, and self-respect and, above all, belief in themselves.

I had a very mixed group most of them serving a life sentence. Suzy was a very small sickly looking young woman who left her mark on me that very day. I had a bucket of fresh roses on my bench and she came over to me and said, "Are these real roses?"

I said, "Yes", thinking to myself, who doesn't recognize a rose? She continued to say "I've never seen a real rose, only in a picture. Can I smell them?"

"Of course you can." I let her take three roses back to her bench to put in a vase and they remained there until they died. She needed to be able to smell those roses with every breath she took that day, and as often as I could make sure it could happen.

I really never forgot this, that there was someone who had not touched or smelled a rose before. I was upset, excused myself for a moment, and went into my office to dry my tears before we continued.

If I Never Touched a Rose

By June Strandberg

Things would have been different,
When I look back and see,
If I never touched a rose
Life would not be the same for me.
I am what I wanted to be
And I did what I feel, that's for sure!
Life can deal its measure of sadness,
But that rose never fails to cure.
As years go by and it's nearing the end,
It was all valuable time that I could spend.
The confidence, my talent, I've been able to share,
If it was only a few women that would have been there.
And from my heart I wanted to show
Just how much I really cared, they needed to know.
And my memory will stay with me for a handful of those
That happened to be fortunate to touch a rose

In memory of dear Suzy

★★★★

An Untitled Poem

Life seems so dull.
The dreary coloured walls,
At night the empty halls,
Screaming to be noticed,
Without attention to oneself.
Days that are unknown of outcome.
What comes next in this place?

Distraught emotions within,
Never actually told.
New and old, so hard for one
To tell the difference from
Where I sit,
Waiting for the untold
Is what goes on in one's head.

Why do we torture?
Because we have to or want to.
Mysteries are the reality here.
How can this be, how
Can one tell real from
Not real?
You cannot because
Everything seems so fake.

You live a life under a microscope
That dissects your whole being.
Who you are,
Stripping one of their true identity.

Get to know us and you would then
Know where there is a person inside
Waiting to be found.

Everyone I know is always wondering
And hoping,
No matter who will care.

Some of us care,
Some of us know the truth.

WE all know who we are and that
NO one can change.

***

Freedom Denied

As I do my dope, like I sometimes do,
I think of the things it's put me through.
The hustling and swindling to get money to buy,
All the attempts at trying to get high.
The depressing sadness of coming right down,
And running right out and going downtown.

I wonder sometimes if it's worth all the trouble,
When the dope can be shitty and price can be double.
The anxiety and stress if you can't seem to score,
But the craving inside you want to do more.
And then there are your friends who have O.D.'d and died
Their lives have been taken, their freedom denied.

***

An Untitled Poem

My soul is crying from the depths within
Trying to find myself, but where to begin?
I guess I begin right from the start
But thinking back just tears me apart.

Don't get me wrong, it wasn't that bad
But now that I'm older I feel very sad.
I can't figure out why I feel this inside.
"Can you help me, will you be my guide?"

Can you give me the way to a happier life?
Help me walk off the blade of this long knife?

I keep thinking to myself, will things ever change?
I have to get a hold and start to rearrange.

I see nothing on this sad and lonely road.
It's long and lonely and I feel very cold.
I need the warmth of true friendship.
I feel like I'm smothering in this 6 by 3 crypt.

I wish someone would hold their arms open
To tell me it's okay, this is what I'm hoping.
All I want is a true and faithful friend
To be there for each other 'till the bitter end.

Chapter Five

When the group of inmates arrived that first day I did not have a contract or funds to outfit my program. With ten thousand dollars of my own funds I brought in design benches, stools, tools, and supplies. We were going to manage without a fridge for a while. Beverly managed to find five thousand dollars that was used to buy flowers. The first day began and I started teaching the women how to make a triangle arrangement. They were given the container for it and shown how to correctly insert the Oasis block that would hold the flowers in place. They took my direction very well and all completed their arrangement. The women were simply overwhelmed that they were able to create this lovely arrangement on their first try. Their next lesson was how to make a boutonniere and they were able to make two or three of them. When the women left that first day I told them to take their arrangements back to their cells and bring them back in the morning with every flower still in place. Not one was to be given away or it would be the last time they would be able to do this. I also mentioned they could take their boutonnieres with them, so they put a pin in each one and away they went, with bouquets and boutonnieres in hand, to the units where their cells were.

It was only fifteen minutes before I had a call from John Pastorek, who was in charge of operations and security. "June, your women have all taken flowers to their units. All the guards are wearing corsages and they have pins in them. We really can't do this so could you get them all back?" I told him they were all going to bring them back, I was just letting them have them for the night to enjoy. I left my office right away to see Beverly in her office and ask her about this. She couldn't see any reason why the women couldn't have the flowers on their units, but she wasn't sure about the boutonnieres on the guards. However, she had a meeting with John and the warden and it was decided that the inmates could have the flower arrangements and the guards could wear a boutonniere if they wanted. That was the day the dynamics of the prison totally changed. At first some of the prisoners were harassing the women in the program, asking what the hell they were doing in there, but that soon stopped when inmates were allowed into the flower shop to buy some. They were able to buy for themselves, fellow prisoners, and family members. Every inmate has a trust account where their money goes for personal needs like cigarettes or chocolate bought from the canteen. They would get paid for any program they attended, schooling they may undertake, or any work they did such as maintenance and gardening, so they would use some of their money for flowers, buying for birthdays, or just to make someone feel good. Anywhere you looked in the prison, from the rotunda to the reverend's office, to the chapel or the teachers' offices, there were flower arrangements. Everywhere you went there were flowers.

My training program covered everything from care and handling of flowers, wedding and funeral etiquette, how to take an order, to work ethics. I told my students there would be no time for tears or bad tempers, and no swearing. So many inmates were from broken families or foster care, many were addicted to drugs or alcohol, had A.I.D.S. or other diseases, But I decided from the onset that I would never let any of this interfere. I did not care about what they did or their illnesses. It was about what they were going to be, everything else was in the past.

I also decided that the arrangements that were being made needed to be sold to people other than the inmates, so every Tuesday and Friday I would take them out to the front entrance and from there the staff would buy them, and in the evening some-times a visitor that had come to see an inmate would buy one. But we had barriers that had to be handled. You could not phone the flower shop directly. The only way you could reach us was through the prison switchboard. We could not be listed in the Yellow Pages under Florists, and we were not in the phone book anywhere.

Burnaby Correctional Centre for Women was a maximum security prison that was located in a remote area next to the Fraser River. On the road leading to the prison you would pass only some vegetable farms and a few warehouses. Beverly was very good about letting people connected to corrections know about us; she was our best public relations person. Another barrier was not having the ability to process credit card transactions for telephone orders. Beverly and I discussed and agreed to contact the Royal Bank of Canada to inquire about the installation of a credit machine. Soon afterwards a lady and gentleman, represen-tatives from the bank, agreed to meet with us. They arrived and the gentleman said, "Just why are we here?" Beverly said we had a floral program in our prison and she turned to me to explain. I said to them that we had a full service flower shop and were plan-ning to expand the business to the outside to build our customer base. We needed a way to process telephone orders and to provide the convenience of credit card purchases for walk up customers, just as every other outside business did. At those words they both looked at Bev and me as if we had just landed from another planet. The gentleman said, "Do you not have women in here that already use Visa, just not their own?" The lady added to this, "The security issues around this request would be dangerous." with that they said they were sorry but this was not going to happen. They got up from their chairs and said no more. With that we saw them to the door.. Bev and I were very disappointed with the outcome, but we were determined this was not going to stop us. Along with the help of John Pastorek, a plan that would convince the skeptical bankers was made and we invited the Royal Bank to a second meeting. This time different representatives arrived and we were able to successfully negotiate being the first prison with credit card capabilities for a prison operated business.

We were ready to roll; one more hurdle overcome. Now I had to put a plan into action so that customers could easily find us and buy our beautiful flowers. We were already successful through our strictly word of mouth marketing, but I felt that we could do even better if we could start to offer wedding floral services.

My floral connections, former customers, and acquaintances knew that if they bought flowers from me, no matter where I was working, I would guarantee my flowers would be the very best. Before very long we were doing weddings. Now I had to go back to John Pastorek and ask him if I could bring brides into our flower shop behind those seven locked doors. He was speechless for a few seconds and said to me, "June, let me take a look at this and see if it's possible." He met with Beverly and the warden and they decided it could happen. Bev could see that the space they had allocated for us was too small and we were moved into a larger area. I was able to obtain moveable display walls from one of our wholesale companies and divided the room into a more spacious flower shop and classroom.

I realized I needed two assistants to help run the flower shop. I hired my daughter-in-law Dana, and my nineteen-year-old daughter Casey to come in and assist me, as she was a great designer and knew the business quite well because she had been raised in it. It was Casey's first day on the job and she had never been inside a prison before. I went out to get her and bring her through to the flower shop, a journey that required a walk through the seven locked doors, but between door five and door six we had to cross through a large rotunda at the same time as inmates were enjoying their coffee break. When we reached door number five Casey could see that there were probably thirty-five or more women sitting around the centre perimeter of the rotunda. She stopped and said, "Mom, I'm nervous to go in there." I assured her it would be okay and that it only took a minute to walk through. As we stepped into the area the whistles started and a few inmates called out to Casey, "How you doing babe?" I think if she could have tunneled her way through she would have started digging on the other side of door number five, but she stood straight with her head held high, walking carefully but quickly with me to door number six. When that door closed and locked behind us Casey looked relieved, leaned up against the door, and took a deep breath. After a few weeks she was finally comfortable taking the long trip through the doors on her own.

While Casey looked after the store with six inmates that had done very well and graduated from the six week basic course and two week wedding course, I started another design course with eight more resident students. I developed a two week horticulture addition to my program that trained inmates in plant propagation and transplantation to the outdoor prison garden and greenhouse. Casey and I chose seeds for flowers we could use in the shop. We worked with a male guard previously trained in horticulture, who built raised beds for all our plants and each summer we grew delphiniums, zinnias, phlox, sunflowers, and other gorgeous flowers. Inmate students were trained to make sure the flowers were always watered and taken care of, and we would go out to weed and fertilize. It worked really well. The women all got along and transformed the prison ground into a place of beauty. The ones that were cleared to go outside the big candy cane perimeter fence planted shrubs and lovely flowers at the front of the prison. It was like no other prison anywhere; inside and out it was changing.

I had to make sure when every student walked out of my class that, first and foremost, they had learned they could hold their heads high, and that their self-confidence was part of their lives they needed to wear each day, no matter what their situation was. Whether waiting for trial, worried about husbands and families, or what might be in store for them, they learned that disasters in life have a way of turning into great stories, teaching us how we can handle the upsets and disappointments. Flowers helped show them how to live life from their hearts and share their sad silence with someone they love and trust.

I knew it was easy for me to give that advice but I wanted to make them understand what it would do for them when they walked into the flower shop for six hours each day and that heavy steel door locked behind them. They had to leave all their unhappiness on the other side, learn peace of mind with flowers all around them, and know they would become beautiful designers with each arrangement they would do and that would make someone else's day wonderful. Worry and unhappiness would interfere with their designing ability.

Let those flowers do their work, let them heal your broken spirit and give you back your soul. You are all the creator's children and you deserve the very best from this day forward. I'm here to make sure that this happens.

It wasn't very long until the guards could see a difference in the women. It made their jobs easier because the inmates were engaged in something they enjoyed and at the same time were gaining marketable skills. Most of the women didn't think they were good for anything.

FEELINGS

I feel alone and lost and empty and in despair.
My ear, head, back and wrists are so sore, it's so unfair.

I feel I need you Lord more than ever before.
My heart is open to you, Jesus, so you can heal and restore.

35

I feel so awake at night and I cannot seem to rest,
My heart is praying and pleading for us and staff to be blessed.

I feel that I am not incarcerated and I am in Rehab Bentery,
My mind and heart are wondering will I be here in the winter.

I feel better after I write a few words of wit.
I will learn from how I feel inside so I can get better bit by bit.

I feel so refreshed after I talk to you, God,
So I am learning to trust you, Lord, instead of "hot Aud."
(*"hot Aud" in this verse means "Acute Use of Drug"*)

I feel and believe God is the almighty, greatest creator of us all,
So I am looking forward to seeing God and
his son Jesus at the golden wall.

I feel a lot better now that I have wrote a few lines,
So I will pray all of us gals and staff and our
families go through clean vines.

I feel the end of time is coming real soon and that life is going
fast,
My heart aches for all who do not know
God, for they will be cast.

★★★★

I HAVE A DREAM

One day I will be free...
free from all,
all the pain,
All the addiction. The addiction is
what caused the pain.

I have a dream...
a dream
That feels like it will never become
a reality.
Just a dream
Can dreams come true?
Can I become true? True to myself?

I have a lot of dreams
But these dreams are only in
my thoughts and reality
When I'm asleep
and actually dreaming.

I had the dream of dreams.

★★★★

Chapter Six

All of a sudden my captive students could hear people saying how beautiful their arrangements were and they would just light up with happiness. It was a sane place for them to be in such dreary, negative surroundings.

As soon as we moved into our new location in the prison I knew the flower shop had to be as close as possible to being like a flower shop on the outside, so I went back to Beverly again to get permission to carry a gift line. This would include a few things that would be safe for the women to be able to buy for themselves or as gifts for their friends or family. She agreed and we brought in fancy soaps, hand creams and lotions, and greeting cards, as well as stationery and a few nice vases for flowers. We began making a few small arrangements with artificial flowers that the students could have in their cells.

There was a ceramic program in a separate area in the minimum security, open living unit of the prison. The ceramic teacher was Jean, a great lady, and a wonderful patient teacher. Any girl on the open living unit who wanted to learn ceramics was given that opportunity. I asked Beverly if we could buy some of their ceramic items that would suit the flower shop. This would be great for us and we would be supporting their program at the same time. Before long Jean had her inmates make beautiful vases and ornamental items suitable for flowers. It was wonderful. They did a lovely job and we in turn could sell them to anyone who came into the flower shop. We carried that lovely line of ceramics for the fourteen years we were there.

★★★

Over all my years as a florist I made it my business to be the very best I could be as a floral designer, floral teacher and floral business woman. I was always involved in the industry in every way. Before I started the prison program I was nominated as Canadian Director of the Northwest Floral Association and continued in that role even after I started work at BCCW. It was important to keep in touch with all the florists I knew in B.C. as I needed all the contacts I could get so I would have job prospects for my students upon their release from prison.

The word traveled quickly through the industry that I had put a florist training program and flower shop inside the prison walls. Some thought I had lost my marbles, others thought I could be a threat to flower shops because I probably sold my flowers cheaper as my students were inmates. Little did they know that I had to educate these florists and my reputation was on the line. Because I was the Director of the Canadian NFA I attended meetings every month that were usually held at one of our wholesalers and included up to forty florists. The NFA had a Board of Directors and we also had our monthly meetings. I decided that my floral colleagues needed to come into the prison and see what kind of work my inmates did and what our flower shop was really all about. They knew I had always been a good floral instructor and put many designers to work in the city wherever I could find a flower shop that needed someone well trained, and that they would be a productive florist from the first day on the job.

At my meeting with the NFA board I mentioned that I had a big enough area between my classroom and the store to have the monthly meetings in the prison, moving the portable walls if I needed more room. They thought this would be a good idea. Very often the board would come to the prison for our monthly meetings and we would use the prison board room. They had all made the trip through the seven locked doors to see the flower shop and were amazed at what existed behind the grey walls.

To get the clearance to have the florist meetings in the prison, I had to first talk to John. As soon as I walked into his office John knew I had another idea that would involve security issues and he would take a deep breath and scratch his head. He said, "What would you like now?" I asked if I could hold my monthly florist meeting in my area. He asked me about how many florists I could expect. I said about thirty to forty usually come. He said he would think about it and make sure all the safety issues were in place and would get back to me if it was going to be possible.

The outside world needed to know how flowers changed this jail. Even the prison psychologist said they had transformed the atmosphere and it was no longer that cold grey place. The flowers created something beyond that.

Every one of those first eight inmates to be trained were all very good, from Suzy to Anita, and they blossomed like the very flowers they were working with. Some of them stayed on in the flower shop to work every day. They were paid a wage that was put in their trust accounts for their needs.

There was another very special young girl in that class who was the same age as Casey, her name was Crystal. She became one of my best and it was also very good because Casey became a role model for these women. They looked up to her and her personality made a difference to them. The atmosphere in the flower shop was happy and everyone got along very well. I always liked background music playing softly, usually light classical, because I found it suited the flowers and was lovely to design to. However, it wasn't very long, only the second day, when one of the inmates turned a rock and roll station on. I was not impressed and told them that there would be no rock and roll, just lovely music to design by, and from that day forward they listened to my music and loved it. Most of them had never listened to this kind of music before in their lives, but they learned that good music and flowers go hand in hand. I also taught them to drop the four letter word from their vocabulary, there would be no swearing in the flower shop.

John finally got back to me and said I could have my florist meeting. I asked permission to have three inmates, who were serving life sentences, demonstrate their floral design skills. Prison officers were somewhat reluctant but my unwavering commitment to my cause won the day. Fifty chairs were set up for the meeting and ninety-eight florists showed up. That was the evening that opened the door as they watched my three designers work their magic.

The outside florists could see that the prices of our flowers were all listed on the chalk board, as they are in any flower shop, and that the prices were the going rate with no special deals. They could also see that Beginnings was not a threat to any one of them. First, our location was remote, we were deep in the heart of the prison behind seven locked doors. Second, we were not allowed to advertise, had no walk-by trade, and at this time didn't even have a refrigerator. However, word of mouth was traveling. The florists that came that night were all impressed with what they saw and told me that when I had a designer being released they would hire them. This is what I needed to hear.

★★★

WOUNDED EAGLE WOMEN

Trapped within this cage
I look down at my wounded

Wings.
Waiting for the strength to
Return.

I wait for the day to fly,
Trapped by my own fears,
Afraid to fly.
Needing to learn to fly
Again

Help me fly, to soar proud.

Chapter Seven

Everyday something new would happen, different experiences, and generally all were positive things.

Before we knew it the local newspaper wanted our story, then a television station wanted to come in, and Floragram invited me to write an article about my program in their magazine. In June, 1993, the Van Dusen Botanical Gardens in Vancouver were holding their first annual Garden in the Park event. This was an outdoor show that brought enthusiastic gardeners to a spectacular fifteen acre public garden to view new ideas in horticulture presented by floral wholesalers, retail flower and garden businesses, and non-profit programs. The organizers provided a very large tent without charge for us, and our inmate designers created beautiful arrangements. Two days before the show opened Casey and I decorated the tent and set up displays of the arrangements. With help from Beverly Roest and her husband Jack, we spent three wonderful days presenting the beautiful work created by women incarcerated in maximum security prison. This event was a huge success that put our program in the public eye, most of whom were unaware that it existed.

We won first prize that year for the best tent display, and even though the women were not there to see it, it was their beautiful arrangements that helped make it what it was. We received lots of praise that day for Beginnings.

It was unfortunate that none of our inmates were eligible for temporary absences at this time, however we had them design every arrangement that went into our beautifully decorated tent. We took lots of photographs so that our inmates were able to see the complete display. We also received wonderful coverage by the Van Dusen Gardens, the Vancouver Sun newspaper and a gardening magazine, so much so that the women were very proud of what they had accomplished inside the prison walls that created an award winning event for Beginnings, an award that belonged to each one of them.

It wasn't long until we started our wedding flower service. John had given us permission to allow brides-to-be to come into the shop to order their flowers. The bride and sometimes a mother or bridesmaid would make their way through the seven locked doors. They would sign in at the prison entrance and our receptionist would call us to bring them through to the flower shop. It was rather daunting for some of them to enter a prison knowing that every time they went through one of those doors they clanked shut and locked. I only had to take one mother back out. As soon as we came through the first door and it locked shut she nearly fainted and said she could go no further. Allowing our customers to come in helped them see what we could do and what a lovely shop we had hidden in the bowels of the prison.

I heard from administration that we had a new Office Manager, Dennis. One morning he called and said, "June, could you come around to my office? I'd like to talk to you about your program." When I entered Dennis' office he started off saying, "I understand you have a floral program in this prison. I also have been told you have an operating flower shop. Where on the outside is the flower shop located? Is it very far from here?"

I was confused that he had not been given correct information but told him, "Our flower shop is located here, in the prison; the training centre and the flower shop are in the same area."

He looked shocked and said, "I'm sure the Attorney General doesn't know he's in the flower business."

I replied, "We've been running the flower shop for nearly two years now." At that moment he had nothing to say to me. I started to leave, turned and said to him, "Maybe you had better phone Mr. Attorney General and tell him he has a flower shop, and if he ever needs flowers to give us a call." With that I left and it was several months later that Mr. Attorney General and a group of government people came into the shop. He looked around and said he thought it was a lovely place, a good program for the inmates to receive a skill, and that they would be pleased to use the flower shop whenever they could. Each one of the gentlemen in the group that day, including the Attorney General, purchased flowers.

Having the Attorney General visit and comment on what a good program we had and how lovely our flower shop was, was very positive. Following this we received more flower orders from different departments of the justice system, also different offices connected to the prison.

The word was out that we would be getting more inmates so I expected some additional students very soon. Beverly advised me that the women's prison at Kingston, Ontario, would be closing with women inmates from British Columbia being transferred to the BCCW, and that I would probably get a few of them in my class. When they arrived I found a much more hardened criminal than what we had previously. Most of them were lifers in for murder or other very serious crimes. One day I was in my office and heard our door unlock. It was after 3:30pm and all my inmate designers had left for the day. I looked up to see two very tall women standing in front of my desk. One was over 6 feet tall. They introduced themselves as Frances and Sherry. Frances said she wanted some artificial arrangements for their apartments (cells). "We want them special and they have to match our colour schemes."

So I said to her, "What colour would that be?"

She answered, "Red and black, and we want them big." Sherry said she wanted a few big arrangements also but hers were to be in shocking pink. Money was no object; they just had to be the best. So the requests were written up and the arrangements were made a bit larger than what we were making for other cells. Beverly allowed them as long as they didn't get in the way in the cells for safety reasons. She told me that Sherry had originally done time in the men's prison. Her name was Billy then but she'd had a gender change and was now a woman. Our horticulture guard had been a guard in the prison where she had started her sentence as a man. Sorry to say, she was such a troubled person. So many things happened to her during the years she was in prison. She tried to commit suicide several times in such terrible ways and was constantly in the infirmary recovering from her attempts. She would cut up her arms until they looked like raw meat. She collected saliva from an inmate that had A.I.D.S, got a rig, and injected into herself. She had a death wish for sure, and finally died very sadly.

Frances stayed on and came to be trained in the floral program and worked in the flower shop. She was one of my favourites, and I felt she could be saved from this life for sure.

Casey and I were cleared to take inmates out on temporary absences for related trips to the floral auction or wholesale design shows. We had both been C-picked and had full security clearance from the first day we walked into the prison. This was not only required for temporary absence escorted trips, but most importantly because we were in and out of the prison every day working side by side with inmates. We were able to take Frances out one day to Central Park, in Burnaby, for a picnic lunch, stopping first at the supermarket to buy what we would eat. Frances had been in prison so long she didn't know that shopping carts had to have money put in them.

Frances was finally going to be paroled and I was worried she wouldn't make it. One thing we were not to do was to see inmates socially or have them as a friend when they left the prison. However, Casey and I broke that rule a bit with Frances. We met her following her release and helped her find a temporary safe place to stay. We then took her to the welfare office to apply for social assistance and help for a more permanent place to live. When she could get settled, I could get her work. Frances seemed to have it together and I felt she would make it. She phoned me one day soon after and said a man she knew met her and offered to help her out. She assured me he would take care of her and she was staying clean -- no drugs. I wanted so badly to believe this. I lost track of her right after that call and didn't hear from her for a long time, but I knew that if I wanted to, the prison grapevine would find her for me. It might take time but they would do this for me.

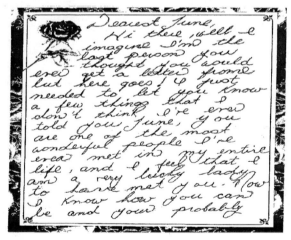

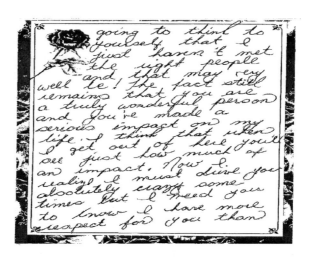

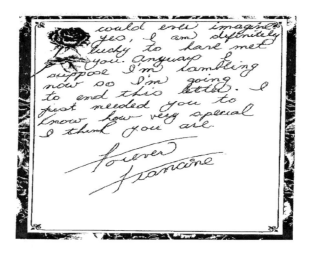

One of my favourite memories of Frances was just before she was paroled she and my inmate staff surprised me with a celebration for my birthday. The prison kitchen baked and decorated a beautiful birthday cake and provided sandwiches and cookies for this special event. The girls asked Casey to bring in balloons and streamers and together they decorated my office. I'll remember that birthday forever.

I have to say I cared about her like she was my own daughter. I wanted to keep her safe. Frances finally got my message and called to say she was okay but somehow I knew she just said this to make me feel good. She didn't want to let me down and called me Mom. As a little girl Frances had been sexually abused and she and her sister had been locked out of their house day after day in the cold winter. They were just little girls with no one to care for them or feed them properly. Their mother was a drug addict and a prostitute. Frances didn't have a chance in her life, and no one to love and take care of her. How can you make it in life when this is all you know? This was the hand she was dealt.

Chapter Eight

The outside community was accepting us more and more. Articles about our beautiful wedding work were written in many magazines. I truly had some of the best designers I have ever seen in my years and I was proud of them.

Every year the CanWest Horticultural Trade Show was held at the luxury Pan Pacific Hotel and received a very large traffic volume, from hotel guests to departing passengers from the adjacent cruise ship terminal. The main entrance of the hotel would be turned into a flower show of arrangements submitted for the People's Choice Awards Competition by fifty to sixty floral designers. Rules were very strict on the height and width of the arrangements, and they were numbered and displayed with the flower shop and designer's name. The public would vote for the first, second, and third design prize.

I told my inmates about the competition and encouraged them to come up with a theme and design something special. I knew they could do it. I would make sure they had all the flowers and supplies required to accomplish their design, including the exact measurements according to the competition rules.

Other designers working in flower shops throughout the Lower Mainland had the opportunity to go to the Pan Pacific Hotel to view where their arrangement would be placed before the competition. My designers did not have that opportunity because they were behind those seven locked doors, so it was up to Casey and I to make sure they were delivered to the hotel and looked perfect.

On the first year entering this competition, three of my best designers, lifers doing time for murder, submitted arrangements and each one was an exquisite work of art and detail. One was a colorful cornucopia with orange, red, yellow, and copper coloured flowers. Foliage spilled out of the front of the cornucopia along with gourds and little pumpkins that were all grown at the prison. Another was a rose pavé creation, an arrangement in which the flowers are arranged in clusters close together to give the appearance of a continuous surface of flowers. Even more intriguing was an arrangement on a wooden base that interpreted an inmate's life situation as a child.

Beverly and John were pleased at our involvement in such a great floral project outside the prison, and even though the inmate designers could not be there in person, their wonderful designs would represent them well. It happened at this time no one qualified for a temporary absence day trip. This was something that had to be earned as well as time served.

Casey and I delivered and set up the arrangements at the hotel. We were so proud of our women: their designs were awarded the first, second, and third prizes, and all received a People's Choice certificate acknowledging what they had done. How very proud they were when everyone in the prison found out what they had accomplished. We knew from then on we would enter that competition each year.

We were always aware that there were protective custody inmates locked away on B-Block and they were very limited in what they could do. It had crossed my mind about what they might be able to help us with up on their unit. Any extra work we might have as it happened.

At a meeting with Beverly I was asked how I felt about teaching the basics of my floral program to inmates on the B-Block protective custody unit. These women were a group of inmates who had committed heinous crimes and were segregated 24/7 and never allowed out into the main population. If they came into the outside courtyard it was when everyone else was locked up. The inmates could not participate in general prison programs, only school courses and crafts that could be done on their secure unit. I agreed and met Sharon, Debbie, Brandie, Vanda, and Marlene and asked if they would be interested in learning about flowers. They were excited about this new prospect, and I knew if I trained them properly they could help us with any extra work I could get, including wedding work.

I started a new program by approaching wholesale floral companies who did piece work and were suppliers of bouquets for some local supermarkets and flower shops. They would produce the assorted arrangements and cut flower bouquets seen in stores, especially at Christmas, Valentine's Day, Easter, and Mother's Day, as well as arrangements for day to day sale. I thought this would be a perfect area for me to expand my prison floral shop business as well as to provide work for the protective custody designers. We would be paid a piece work rate with funds going toward the program. The wholesalers were very interested in my plan and shipped various style prototypes and all required flowers and supplies needed to produce these arrangements. We started with the Christmas season and continued with special occasion arrangements for Mother's Day, Valentines, Easter, and Christmas for quite a few years.

Those women on B-Block couldn't believe they were going to be able to be part of the flower program. They completed the arrangements for Christmas that would be going to all the retail outlets who wanted them. The designs they made were the Christmas arrangements featured by FTD (Florists' Transworld Delivery), Teleflora, and the American Floral Service. The women did a wonderful job and their perfect arrangements were put on the auction carts and picked up at the prison by truck, then taken to the wholesalers, who were only a few blocks away.

After I involved the B-Block inmates in my floral program, and found it to be very successful, John Pastorek then decided to try bringing the protective custody women down for training in my classroom next to the flower shop. This could cause problems for my regular inmates, who were trained and had jobs in the flower shop. They knew the prison population would be up in arms that regular inmates could be mixing with PCs, something prisoners were very much opposed to. I had to explain the plan to them, that they would come into the flower shop before the PCs were escorted by guards to the training room. They would be confined there while I trained them, not leaving until the regular inmates had left the flower shop at the end of each day.

This new project the prison was trying worked and was finally accepted by everyone. The protective custody inmates became great designers and, because they were all doing life, I knew I would have staff for as long as they wanted to work for us.

During training, Sharon and Debbie, two of the PCs, got into a terrible fight. On each design bench there were heavy metal holders that we kept different gauges of wire in. Each one of them had one in their hands and headed toward each other ready to swing. Debbie got the first blow that caught her on the forehead and blood started to flow. However, before I could get between them she landed a hit on Sharon. It was a nasty scene, but, between Casey and I, we were able to get them under control. Dana, my daughter-in-law, rushed to my office to call control and there was a guard at our door in short order. Sharon and Debbie were escorted out and immediately put into 24/7 segregation, where they stayed until their differences were solved. As we had reached the end of our class that week, Sharon and Debbie were not allowed to return, however they continued to design for me from their unit.

Chapter Nine

I would always try to bring in different items for sale in the flower shop. Since the prison administration was allowing the inmates to have flowers, plants, and artificial arrangements in their cells, I decided I would bring in some nice dried foliage and decorative branches like curly willow, wheat, huckleberry branches, and poppy pods. I was leaving the prison one day and had to pass the Senior Corrections Officer's office. He called me in and asked me to look at something they had found in one of the cells. It was an ice cream bucket filled with murky brown water with seeds floating on the top. He said, "June, do you recognize this?"

I looked closer and could see it was poppy seeds. I was very surprised but said, "They're poppy seeds." I was a bit innocent and didn't know what you could do with these.

He continued. "The inmates bought these pods from you, put them in water, and cooked them in the microwave on their unit, and then hid them in one of the cells." They were able to do this while the unit guard was in her office processing paperwork and, even though she had full view of the unit, she had missed the poppy stew being made. The prisoners thought they would get a high from this murky drink, but little did they know the seeds were all dried out and hollow so they were no good to them. It didn't work. However, the SCO suggested I not bring the poppy pods in again. It was peculiar because every time I had brought them in they sold like hotcakes. I thought I had a winner there.

I found out later that the inmates who worked in the kitchen would smuggle potato peels and also any fruit they could lay their hands on. All fruit was counted on the units so it wasn't always easy for them to get it. All of these ingredients went into jail house brew. Inmates were so good at planning this and their strategy was unique to say the least, but finally the guards would get to know that there was brew percolating somewhere in that prison. A complete sweep would be done of the units; the gym, the workout room, out in the greenhouse, and the horticulture building. Everywhere was searched until the brew was found and done away with, but it wasn't very long until there would be another brew cooking.

Another slick thing the inmates were really good at was getting drugs into the prison; there was good money to be made. The inmate who would use the drugs would get a relative or friend to put money in their trust account thinking it would be used for a legitimate purpose, but in exchange for the drugs the inmate pusher would receive that money or cigarettes in their trust account.

You would think it would be difficult to get drugs into a prison, but they knew every way it could be done. Sometimes when they had a visit from someone on the outside that was cleared to come in and meet face to face in the visitor's lounge, for example if an inmate's boyfriend or husband came in, he may have a package of coke wrapped up in a small plastic bag that he would keep in his mouth. Just as he was about to leave he would kiss the inmate on the mouth and pass the package from his mouth to hers.

Some inmates were allowed temporary absences and would go out for a day with a relation or cleared friend. Before they would return they would score drugs and make sure they were suit cased (that means the drugs were inserted inside their bodies and kept there until they were safely back in their cells). Cavity searches were never done upon return, only pat downs. The inmates were allowed street clothing to be brought in to them. The guards would go over the clothing as closely as possible, but often the drugs were missed. The person that had brought the clothes in may have picked open a seam or the hem on a pair of jeans, inserted the drugs, then carefully sewed up the open space so that no one would spot the contraband, nor would it fall out.

Other ways were a lot less sneaky. There was a big courtyard surrounded by a very tall candy cane steel fence. At night, after the guards had done their last perimeter inspection, someone on the outside would sneak up through the trees and, where the lights were not shining down, they would throw the drugs over the fence to land exactly where they had told the inmate it would be. The first inmate out there in the morning would have been told and they would retrieve the drugs before any guards or the horticulture instructor came outside.

Piercings and tattoos were another thing that was done inside, ever so crudely, but done regardless. Brandie, an inmate from B-block, was a tattoo artist and really good at piercing.

Having a tattoo has been on my bucket list for many years and I spoke of it several times while I was running my prison program. Brandie said she would be pleased to do my tattoo, however, as nice as it was for her to offer, I decided to pass. Another thing I was getting ready to do was get a second ear piercing. She heard me mention that and told me she could take care of it really easily. Ice cubes, a cork, and a sharp needle were all I had to scurry up. Again I thanked her and said I had decided not to do it. I did get it done but on the outside by a professional. There wasn't anything they didn't offer to do, or want to get me, but I would say thank you very much and let them know I was fine and could manage to get the things I needed. That didn't stop them from offering. It was never about what they could get out of me. They showed me respect at all times and in their own way they cared and wanted to do any favours they could for me.

Patricia, a woman in her forties who had served quite a bit of time in Kingston Prison, was finishing her sentence at BCCW. She was one of my resident staff inmates in the flower shop, an excellent worker and nice designer. She was due to go out on a three day temporary absence, a reward that was earned first by good behaviour in prison, and by the length of her sentence. The inmate had to be accompanied by an escort, who had been cleared to take her out to a destination that had also been checked and considered safe. Just before she left she came into my office and asked me if there was anything she could get me; my favourite perfume, or a Louis Vuitton purse perhaps? I thanked her for thinking of me but told her I was well fixed for perfume and wasn't fond of Louis Vuitton purses. I didn't ask any questions, but I wondered how she would be able to obtain these. Both were very expensive and I was sure she didn't have that kind of money.

Most of the inmates that I had over the years would share their stories with Casey and me, often giving every last detail of their crime, and always their sad lives from beginning to end. Patricia told how she had committed the crime that landed her in jail. There was Leanne, another beautiful designer doing time for being found guilty of hot capping (giving bad drugs to) someone that caused their death. There were three more beautiful young women inmates, Rhonda, Marsha, and Doreen, who came into the flower program. All three were in their early 20s and came from good family backgrounds, were beautiful, had good manners, and were well groomed. Where did they go wrong, what happened? They were well educated, always polite and well spoken, and just didn't fit into this scene. Two of them let the wrong man into their lives, and one went travelling to Thailand.

Rhonda met the wrong man and was in on a murder charge. Marsha broke into a house with her boyfriend, not knowing there was someone at home: a young, pregnant mother whom they kept hostage but took good care of. However, it still brought a stiff sentence for them. Doreen travelled to Thailand and was caught on a drug related crime that brings the death penalty in that country. The Canadian government was able to get her transferred back to Canada, but only if she was given a life sentence. She was serving it at BCCW.

Rhonda was our number one wedding designer, Marsha won at the People's Choice Awards, and Doreen was another top wedding designer. These three women worked with us for most of the time they were in the prison.

We were taking more than one hundred wedding orders each year and were so busy that I brought the protective custody women back down to the classroom and trained them for wedding work. On completion they returned to their unit on B-Block, where they did all the piece work and wedding work that we could send up to them.

★★★

LOST

I am lost and lonely and so far from everything in here.
I try to understand it before it all ends in fear.

I am lost and lonely and so far from all my family and friends.
I try so hard to keep busy so I don't go over the deep end.

I am lost and lonely and so far from healing my past sexual abuse.
I try so much to understand and let go so I will not blow a fuse.

I am lost and lonely and so distant from enjoying God's blessings.
I try too hard I guess, that's why I'm always guessing.

I am lost and lonely and so confused about what has happened to
me.
I try not to blame myself, but no one hears my plea.

I am lost and lonely and wondering how long I will get yet.
I try not to worry, but how do I try to forget.

I am lost and lonely and sorry, I promise Jesus will set me free.
I try to understand you, God, but sexual abuse has a grip on me.

I am lost and lonely and frustrated about how the medical system
treats us inmates.
I try to make excuses for the medical staff
so they will see the pearly gates.

I am lost and lonely and far from healing. I am distant and confused.
Wandering and sorry and frustrated, I am lost and lonely.

Chapter Ten

One day Beverly phoned me and asked me to come and see her. She said she had an idea, already discussed with John, that she wanted to put to me to see what I thought.

Brandie was one of the PCs doing life for murder and had been transferred to B.C.C.W from she Kingston Penitentiary. Brandie had made a request to come down to the flower program to work. She was already trained, was a top designer, and her attitude had changed. I realized she was one of the most dangerous inmates in the prison but I had to believe that those flowers and this program had made a big difference to her. I couldn't allow what she had done to cloud my judgement on what or how she might change. She would be a PC working with my regular inmates. Could we do it, would it work? Everyone in the prison knew her, even though she was locked away on B-Block; her reputation was well-known.

Casey and I gathered our women together and talked about what the plan was for Brandie. She would come in every day and be in the program with them in the same room standing beside them designing. What did they think of this? Well, they were opposed to say the least, but again we asked them if they would give it a try temporarily to see how it went. Their biggest worry continued to be how they would be treated by the other inmates when they found out they were working side by side with a PC who was looked down on mainly because PC crimes were the worst of crimes. Certainly Beverly and John knew the ramifications and would never put inmates' safety at risk, but the PCs had already been trained in the flower program in the same room with the regular inmates.

It would also be a risk for Brandie coming through the prison when some of the population could be on the move at the same time. Over the next few days the women in the flower program talked to Casey and me, individually expressing their concerns. However, to my surprise each one was willing to give it a try. We said that if, for any reason, they were too uncomfortable, or any of the other inmates made threats to them in any way, they must advise us and we would change the situation. Everyone knew Brandie, and they knew she had a lot of influence with other inmates, not just on B-Block. There could be repercussions if anyone did something that she didn't approve of.

Brandie started almost right away. Every day she was escorted from B-Block to the flower program with a guard, who would return to escort her back to her cell at the end of the day. She was already attended by an escort generally, following her movements with the other inmates going to their programs. All went well and before we knew it everyone in the room was working very well together. Brandie respected how everyone felt about her and was grateful that the women in the flower program were willing to take a chance with their own safety with other inmates and accept her as one of the design staff in the program. Another first: a PC working in a program with regular inmates. However, quite a while later there was a very serious incident involving Brandie in the rotunda, a place where all inmates could sit on their spare time and visit with one another. A young inmate was stabbed while she sat in the rotunda with other inmates during a coffee break. She survived but was injured quite seriously. Immediately there was a lock down and inmates were sent back to their units. The rotunda has cameras positioned in such a way that the guards in control can keep a close eye on everyone there and all their movements. Immediately after this incident the camera footage was scrutinized by John, the Principal Officer, and the Senior Corrections Officer to see what they could detect on how the stabbing had taken place. They could see Brandie coming through the rotunda on her way to health care. She stopped and spoke to another old-time inmate, then continued on her way. They never really knew where the knife came from; it was hard to prove how the inmate that did the stabbing got it, and no inmate would say anything to incriminate another, but it appeared that there may have been six or seven inmates involved in the incident. Brandie was kept on B-Block for approximately six weeks until the investigation was completed. As a result a lot of privileges were taken away. It was difficult to prove how and when Brandie had taken the knife, but they were sure it came from the flower shop. Protocol was changed after this and when an inmate left, if only for a minute, their tools had to be accounted for.

Brandie was also on drug watch a lot because she was a user. Prison administration used the 'piss test' quite often and would do this with the inmates that they suspected of using drugs. They never knew how Brandie got her drugs in, but there was word on the grapevine that it was her dear mother that brought them to her during visits. She must have been very good at hiding the drugs on herself and then passing them over to Brandie without being detected, she was never caught.

Time went on, day after day, and there was always something different; drama, heartache and sadness, suicide attempts, drug smuggling, theft, and on and on. This didn't happen in the flower shop, it always seemed to be on the other side of door number seven.

FOREVER ALWAYS

Here I sit, sad and blue.
I lost something that once was true.
In my heart I feel the pain,
But my Lord I have something to gain.

You picked me up when I was down
And made me stand on solid ground.
I thought I had something gold
And wishing together we'd grow old,
But along the line we grew apart
Hoping only for a better start.

You are the one I hold so true
And though at times you made me blue
I hurt, I weep, I cry, I bleed.
Deep inside you're all I need.
Your love I've held so long,
Where my love did we go worn.

You're all I held inside my heart,
Hoping only we'd never part.
Your touch, your smile, your hopes and fears.
Now I'm alone, reduced to tears.
Hoping you'll come and take my hand
And take me to that Promised Land.

Chapter Eleven

A new group of women came into the prison, some long termers, some shorter, but mostly doing time for various serious crimes. We had a couple of women from the USA who had been charged in Vancouver and had to do their time in Canada. One was a large, boisterous woman named Chantel, the other was Madeline, a very small and dainty lady, who was beautiful and very well dressed.

Madeline was not very keen on being in the flower program but by the time she had been trained in basic and advanced floral design, plus wedding work, she was hooked. She became another outstanding designer.

The word was traveling fast about my designers and the Vancouver Art Gallery phoned about their new showing titled 'Art and Flowers'. They were interested in knowing if any of the inmates would like to participate and I certainly thought this was a wonderful opportunity for them. Casey and I went to the gallery, where they explained they had three pictures that would need arrangements to match the colours and also depict what the pictures were about. We took a camera thinking we could take a photo of the art so that our designers would know what was expected, but this was not allowed because the pictures were original art works.

On a piece of paper I quickly sketched an outline of each picture with notes on colour and detail, took them back to my inmates, and did my best to convey what I'd seen so they could do their arrangements to match. Other florists from throughout the city who were submitting arrangements were able to go to the gallery to see the painting they had to design around but my designers didn't have that luxury, however they each created their design and Casey and I took their arrangements to the art gallery. You would have thought my inmate designers had viewed their picture; their arrangements matched to perfection. The art committee in charge of the displays couldn't believe their eyes at what an outstanding job they all did. Casey and I had made sure the inmates chose the right flowers and correct colour. The gallery was so impressed that they asked me when we returned for our containers if we would come back next year, and we did. The following year, not only did we get five pictures to do, we were asked to interpret the gallery's main entrance picture. It was the 8' x 5' famous black and white picture of Marilyn Monroe wearing her long string of pearls and her beautiful elbow length white satin gloves, and holding a champagne glass in front of her. Casey and I again studied the pictures and told the designers that the one in the lobby was a challenge. Madeline stepped up and said, "I'll do it." And do it she did. We borrowed two tall pillars from our wholesalers, who also gave us a gorgeous, very large vase resembling a huge champagne glass that stood at least 3' high and was very wide at the top, and another beautiful glass vase. Madeline created two awesome arrangements with red roses. We found her a Christmas garland that resembled a string of pearls, and we were also able to find long satin gloves at the Salvation Army Thrift Store. The arrangement was absolutely breathtaking. Everyone was astounded at what this young woman locked away in a maximum security prison was able to do without seeing the picture. She literally had seen it through our eyes. She created it and made a name for herself. We were so very proud of all the arrangements, each one was beautiful and matched the pictures perfectly.

The women were all doing so well and involving them in the outside world gave them such confidence despite obstacles that would cross our path, and things that were difficult for us to do because our flower shop was behind bars. John, Director of Operations, and Beverly backed me every step of the way. Safety was first and foremost so when I would approach them with another idea that involved the other side of that big fence and seven locked doors, they would check everything out and make sure it would all work within the guideline of prison protocol and safety.

My next venture was to ask John and Beverly if I could have a Christmas open house. I wanted to be able to let all our customers, friends, and the public be allowed to come into our flower shop. My plan was to involve all the prison programs; the tailor shop, beauty shop, ceramic program, and any inmate that had made hand-crafted items.

I wanted to decorate the flower shop like any flower shop with Christmas decorations and with a good selection of Christmas gifts. I asked Sharon, the tailor shop instructor, what she could do and because she was a great instructor and felt it was a good idea for us all to be a part of the open house, she had her inmates make Christmas stockings, pretty aprons, children's pyjamas, colourful cozy throws, book bags, t-shirts, and more. The beauty parlour was going to sell beauty products and the ceramic program would bring all their beautiful ceramic ornaments, including vases and mugs hand-painted by the ceramic students. The kitchen baked shortbread, Christmas loaves, and tarts. The inmates brought any crafts they had made, from knitting and crochet items to jewelry.

John made sure it could work safely. We were at the very back of the prison, directly across from the tailor shop, and they could close off the prison from door number six. This way the tailor shop and the flower shop could spring their doors and we also had the hallway to use. There was a door that led to the outside enclosed delivery area as well as another door that led out to the greenhouse and horticulture centre. We had freshly made Christmas wreaths and door swags, which we displayed in the greenhouse. Our horticulture instructor lit a pathway with Christmas lights all the way to the greenhouse so that customers could make their way out there. He also had small Christmas trees planted in pots for sale. His staff made wooden reindeer that would hold a poinsettia. The beauty parlor set up their table in the tailor shop. Ceramics, inmate crafts, and kitchen baked goods came into the flower shop.

Beverly arranged with New Haven, the men's open living maximum security prison on Marine Drive to prepare hors d'oeuvres that we could serve our customers. A table was set conveniently by the exit doors where the customers paid administration staff overseeing cash and credit transactions. All items for sale were clearly marked so that programs received their money accurately. Each program had two or three of their student inmates cleared to work at the open house. They wore red t-shirts made in the tailor shop that had Beginnings written on the front to make them easy to spot and keep track of amongst the customers.

We sent invitations to our former customers and others in any way connected with, or that knew about, our prison programs. As open house customers arrived through the gated area to the door that led into our section, a guard would check their name off the list, and as they left they would be checked again. The event was a huge success and some 350 people came to shop and enjoy the evening. Each of the inmates that were cleared to be at the open house were well behaved and waited on each customer with confidence. All conducted themselves very professionally.

Again I went to Beverly to ask permission for Casey and me to take some of our best inmate designers, that were allowed temporary absences at the time, to the florist wholesalers for their annual Christmas Design Show, where professional florists demonstrate how to design with the wide array of product available at the wholesale level.

This was something I did for the wholesalers for quite a number of years. I thought if the inmates attended before our Christmas Open House it would inspire them even more. Casey and I had been cleared to take prisoners out on temporary absences. Permission was granted, then I asked to have seven of my best designers cleared to attend. They were all approved and away we went. It was a wonderful day and the inmates thoroughly enjoyed the experience and learned a lot. It was a great opportunity for them to be able to mix with other florists. Eyes were on us when we entered the warehouse but we didn't worry about that. I had phoned the wholesalers with my plan and was assured there would be no problems.

Chapter Twelve

Another year rolled around for the CanWest People's Choice Awards and the inmates were excited to enter the competition again in 1993. Brandie was entering for the first time and decided she wanted to decorate a large galvanized garbage can. She knew exactly how it was to be. Martin, the horticulture instructor, was able to give her a new garbage can from supplies. According to her plan, he cut some pieces out of the can and dented it to make it look old. She gathered empty tins from the kitchen, and anything we had that was going in the trash that would work for her. She proceeded to glue the trash items throughout her garbage can very artistically. The arrangement had to be 75% flowers, so she used red gladiolus, red carnations, two-tone red and yellow roses; all beautiful colours and choice of foliage. When you first looked at her completed design you noticed there was trash falling out of the can, but as you got closer, all of a sudden there was a beautiful colorful arrangement of fresh flowers bursting up from the bottom. It was something beautiful coming out of a can of thrown away trash. To me she was sending a message. She gave her arrangement the title:

"Something Beautiful can come from Something Thrown Away and Forgotten".

Most of the inmates felt like they were discarded and forgotten with no hope for anything good for them in the future, but when they walked through door number seven, they soon found a new beginning. Something beautiful surrounded them every day that they could touch, smell, see, and experience the beautiful feeling flowers put inside them. For the first time in some of their lives they found out how special they were and that there was a life worth living, for there could be a light at the end of their long dark tunnel.

There was something in our flower shop that was nowhere else in the prison. It was nothing I or Casey or Dana did; it was the beautiful flowers and the magic spell they created for each and every one behind locked door number seven. Life behind bars as they knew it changed. During our fourteen years at BCCW many lost and broken souls were healed working with flowers. No one is born bad!

Brandie's trash can was a huge success at the People's Choice Award. She placed second, which was something that had never happened to a protective custody inmate, especially one doing life for more than one murder. She had set a great example. Before Brandie became a part of the floral program they could hardly get her out of bed. She would stay locked up for twenty hours every day, but her outlook soon changed. She found the program uplifting and said it gave her freedom to express herself. In the year that she came to work with me, Brandie added no new scars to the hundreds that disfigured her forearms.

As time went on I was able to have several of the inmates cleared to go to the floral auction with Casey and me. We would pick them up at 5:30am for the United Flower Growers morning auctions held only blocks from the prison. When our floral purchases were loaded into our van we would visit our wholesalers to purchase our supplies. This gave the inmates an insight into how the florist business world operated, and they were thrilled to participate.

Quite a bit of time had lapsed since Frances had been paroled, I had not had any calls from her, and over time we lost track of her. We were in the middle of getting the women ready to prepare their arrangements for the CanWest People's Choice Awards when the door intercom buzzed to gain entry to the flower shop. It was Frances who was back inside for a parole violation, and she came in as if she had never been away, asking us how we all were and what was new. I told her we were getting ready to enter arrangements to the People's Choice Awards. She lit up and said she wanted to enter, I looked at her and told her it was only two days away.

"I can pull that off, no problem," she said. And I knew she could. I told her to draw up a diagram, keeping the measurements in mind, and to give me a list of supplies she would need.

We had a wooden 36" base with 3" sides all round left over from a few years prior, so this was her start. Frances' list included a small rubber tire off a tiny bicycle, a little shoe, and a small teddy bear. She needed a sturdy tree branch, some sand, and her flowers. Martin secured the tree branch from the bottom and gave her the sand. About 3" from the outside edge, on two sides of the perimeter of the inside of the box she secured her oasis pieces. She made a little fence of bamboo and wire that went in front of the oasis, sand covered the bottom. Next, Frances inserted grass like foliage into the oasis around the fence, then placed all her flowers as if they were growing along the fence line. In the middle was the tree branch with a little tire swinging from it, and in the sand lay one little running shoe, the small teddy bear, and a little pink ribbon. The title she gave her arrangement was, "Lost, but not Forgotten". The message said a little girl had been taken but they would never forget her. She tied yellow crime scene tape around the design.

Casey was in charge of all submissions to that year's People's Choice Awards and saw the reactions of those who looked at this arrangement. On every arrangement the designers name and the flower shop she represented was displayed, so people saw that she was from Beginnings in the women's prison. The arrangement touched a lot of people. It told Frances story, how lost she was, and how she found out that we cared about her and we were lucky to have found her. She left a mark in my life. I will never forget her.

We kept entering the women into as many floral competitions as we could. The next major one was in the showrooms of one of the largest wholesalers and was sponsored by one of the large suppliers. Each florist had to make an arrangement and take it to the wholesaler, where they were to be on display for the whole day. Each designer who entered an arrangement was to be there standing at their table to answer any questions about their display. There was a good crowd of florists that came that day and the organizers announced that the young lady that had done one particular arrangement could not be there because she was in an inmate designer at Beginnings. Instead I stood behind her arrangement and answered the questions. The tablecloth on her table received at least a dozen or more florist's signatures, saying what a lovely arrangement she had made. There were also messages of job offers for when she was released.

More and more florists would call me to see if I had anyone coming out that would need work. This was wonderful because it meant I could make sure the inmates had work upon their release. I was always careful to place them with the right florist. As soon as they were settled on the outside they would be in touch with me and with their parole officer, and I also usually knew from their case worker inside the prison where they were going, generally to a safe house or a registered rehabilitation centre. Sometimes they were returning home to a family member and I would do my best to find them a job close to where they were living, or on a direct transportation route.

Chapter Thirteen

I was Canadian Director of the Northwest Florists' Association at the time it was the British Columbia Chapter's turn to host the annual convention. We held it at the Whistler Ski Resort. Many floral arrangements were required for the luncheons, breakfasts, dinners, President's Ball, as well as the host hotel's lobby, restaurant, and VIP suites. Any florists that were attending the convention were welcome to volunteer to design and were recruited to help out, but the designs for the main theme arrangements for the many different functions had been designed earlier. Prototypes were prepared before we left Vancouver and would be copied once in Whistler.

Different florists offered their designs to suit each function. Of course my designers at the prison also submitted their designs. Out of the fifteen submissions, eight of my designer's bouquets were chosen, with the most important being done by Anita for the President's Ball.

There was a large luncheon on one of the days that required thirty-six table arrangements and it was one of ours that had to be copied. It happened that the inmate that created that arrangement prototype was Madeline, my art gallery designer. Even though she was still serving time, she was a model prisoner and was being allowed periodic temporary absences as she was getting closer to release. I wanted to be able to take her with me Whistler and we would be gone from Thursday afternoon until Monday. I went to Beverly to ask if I could take her. There would be Casey, a florist friend Carol, myself, and hopefully Madeline all staying together in a suite at the hotel. Beverly checked everything out and said she could go. So away we went in our van the four of us. Madeline was so excited to be a part of this and so were we.

When we arrived at Whistler the hotel told us where we could do the designing. Wally, a floral designer friend of mine, and I were in charge of the flowers, all the designs for the dinners, and others, including the big design show.

The large luncheon where our thirty-six table arrangements were to be used would be made in the convention centre itself, and Madeline was the designer I put there to complete them. It was her prototype so she knew exactly how the arrangement was to be done. The rest of us continued to design in the hotel. Later that day the manager of the convention centre asked me, "Who is the young lady that is working over there?" I told him she was my designer. "Does she work for you?" I said yes. He asked, "Would she be interested in a job? Would she consider working for us up here?" I thought to myself, my God she's an inmate doing time. He said, "We are about to hire a designer for our convention centre. She is just what we need and could oversee that for us. Would you be willing to let her go from your business?" I told him I would need to get back to him.

When we returned to the prison I presented Madeline's job prospect to her case worker, as she was soon to be paroled. Following protocol and a great deal of consideration, the prison allowed Madeline to take the job in Whistler on a part-time basis to evaluate how responsible she would be. She would leave the prison each Thursday afternoon, travel by train to Whistler, and return each Sunday. It would be necessary to find accommodation for her that would have security clearance.

Now I had to phone the Whistler Convention Centre manager and give him the full details, and to advise him that the situation was more complicated than what he would expect. I provided information on Madeline's work ethic in the prison flower shop as well as the need to find appropriate accommodation for her there. To my surprise he didn't care about Madeline's prison record, and did not ask why she was in prison; it was not up to me to tell him. It would be up to Madeline to tell him if he asked her. He mentioned that the dentist in town and her husband were personal friends, and they had a small suite in their basement that he knew they would be pleased to rent to Madeline for the days she required. He was also positive about giving Madeline more work once she had finished serving her time.

The dentist and her husband met Madeline and they were cleared to let her stay in their home from Thursday to Sunday. This placement worked very well. Madeline completed her sentence and moved permanently to Whistler. The following year she married and moved on to a full-time position in a gift store with a flower shop, and to this day lives in the Whistler area and has a successful life.

You must live your life from your heart. That's exactly what she did.

Chapter Fourteen

This is another sad story around one of our best designers who was with us in the flower shop for about five years. Crystal and Casey, who were about the same age, got along and worked very well together. Crystal was very pretty and she looked up to Casey as a role model. She too had almost completed serving her time. Over the years, as young as she was, she had been in and out of prison from juvenile detention, to minimum, and then maximum security. Addicted to drugs on the outside and inside the prison, she scored when she could. Finally she turned the corner with the help of her case worker, health care personnel, the beauty parlor instructor who cared about her, as well as Casey, Dana, and me. She cleaned up and served the balance of her time drug free, and I knew I could get her work. She also had good strong support in her family. The day came and she was released from prison. Out only two days, she was found dead from an overdose. The word in the prison from some of the inmates was that it happened to her on purpose, she did not take her own life. This was especially sad because she was definitely ready to start her life over.

There was a special arrangement that Crystal had made and that meant so much to all of us. It was a small, blue, antique wire bird house. She put a very pretty dried arrangement inside just under the little perches, and wired the little door open so it couldn't be closed. That's how she felt. She was that little bird that had nested in a bed of flowers, caged, but it was time to fly away. We put a small card on it, "In Memory of Crystal". The day I got the news of her death was one of the saddest days I had in the prison. She was young, beautiful, and just got on the wrong path years before. There were lots of obstacles on her way. Somehow she had been able to get through it all.

You need to share your sad silence with someone you love to help you make it through the dark times in your life.

A Poem

FOR CRYSTAL

Though I never knew you well,
These feelings so deep, I must tell.
Showing on your friends' faces,
Pain and loss leaving their traces.

The reason for their sorrow,
For with you Crystal... never again
to share tomorrow

As together, their prayers never cease,
For you Crystal, to rest in peace
...........Forever...........

For you, Crystal.

There were happy times and sad times. You had to be able to understand this when you worked in such a desperate place. You think it would be easier each time something serious happened, but it never got any easier, it just put another little void in your heart. All I ever wanted to do was make them all better, to take care of them when they were with us and try to make sure they were safe upon their release. Beverly once said to me, "June, we're really glad you don't have the key for the front door, or you would let them all go home."

I knew very soon while working inside the prison that I needed to have a program on the outside that released inmates could go to if needed. I worked on plans for a recovery house that had a place for them to live and have a flower shop all on the same site. I would train them, they could stay and work, and when they were strong and ready I would find them work in another flower shop once they were settled. I felt this could work. I did my best to start the process while I was at BCCW. Casey and I looked at different places that we thought would work, and found a beautiful heritage home that had been a restaurant and was now for sale. It had wonderful living accommodations on the top floor. I wanted my new endeavour to be a coffee house and flower shop, and this would be a perfect setting. It was large enough to accommodate eight women.

There was a grant coming up for projects such as this so we submitted our proposal. We were awarded the grant but it had loop holes that stood in our way. There was a deadline to have all the paperwork and permits together, but I needed to go to the New Westminster City Hall and have a meeting with the council to get permission to have a recovery residence and flower shop for released inmates. It would have to be approved with the best interests of the community. It was just the start of the summer break so I knew I wouldn't be able to get it all completed. We had already met with the real estate agents and they said we could lease the property. It would have been a perfect place, but it wasn't meant to be. We looked at other locations during that summer but we had to finally accept that we were unable to meet the criteria within the allotted time, so my proposal got filed away for the time being. It was supposed to be that way because I needed to always give one hundred percent at the prison. Even though my plan on the outside included trained employees to help, I would have had to be involved and it would interfere with my job at BCCW.

But even though it didn't happen right then, I knew someday I would make it happen, and even though we were disappointed at the time, it was for the best. We carried on with business as usual at the prison, teaching the program to a new group of inmates three times a year.

We continued to provide floral services for over one hundred weddings a year. I had the best designers any flower shop could ask for, and our reputation was top notch. Brides would put the word out about how beautiful our wedding flowers were, and prospective brides would each walk through the seven locked doors to our shop to order their own.

Chapter Fifteen

Brandie was still working and doing a lovely job of her wedding bouquets. She came to me one day and asked if she could meet with a bride and take the wedding order from her. A request like this needed approval from the prison program director and head of operations, but in a few days the decision was made to allow Brandie's request, with a few prerequisites.

Casey or I were to advise the bride-to-be before she came into the flower shop that an inmate would be taking her order and inquire if she would be comfortable with that. We were never to leave our customers alone with the inmate. Brandie was also required to change her appearance. For example, she had to get rid of her orange hair colour and remove the piercings in her nose, lip, tongue, and eyebrow. She could only keep her ear piercings while dealing with customers. Her arms were badly damaged from self-mutilation, so I advised her to borrow a long sleeved blouse and come to work dressed as she would if going to work in a flower shop on the outside. She made all the changes we required and she looked great on her arrival in the flower shop to work as a wedding floral consultant. I was very pleased. Brandie was a protective custody inmate that had committed serious crimes, she had a foul mouth and was a drug addict, and all-in-all a dangerous woman. She made a complete change, was polite and respectful to others, and was careful not to swear while in the flower shop. She was also a beautiful floral designer.

In a 1993 interview with a journalist from the British Columbia Women's Magazine, Brandie explained how flowers had opened up a new world for her. She talked about how living in jail, and especially in protective custody, made her feel uptight, but when she would come into the flower shop her outlook changed and gave her the freedom to express herself. She said, "Without Casey and June, and the flower program, the prison would be a real horrible place to be. When things get tough or you really feel down and you just feel like saying 'to hell with everything', you don't because you don't want to let June down. We all feel very committed to her. She goes all out for us; she's like our family."

I went to escort Brandie's first customer to the flower shop. Upon explaining that their order would be taken by an inmate, I was happy to immediately receive assurance that the bride, her mother, and her bridesmaid were just fine with this arrangement. Brandie took her first wedding order that day, writing down each detail to perfection, and helping the bride make the right decisions with flowers and colours. When they were about to leave, the bride and mother thanked her so much for all her help to make this day for the young bride so special. When they were leaving the flower shop they each gave Brandie a big hug. She had tears to even think someone would not only let her wait on them, but give her a big hug too. It had never happened before and was a first for a protective custody inmate anywhere, in any jail, ever. Brandie worked very hard, following through with this order right up to the wedding day, making by herself all the bouquets, corsages, boutonnieres, and flowers for the church and reception. She even received permission to come back to the flower shop after dinner to finish it all up. Casey and I were there working so she stayed with us until everything was completed.

That bride and groom sent her a wonderful thank-you card and letter, telling her how special she had made their day with her beautiful flowers. That meant more to Brandie than anything she had ever received in her life and was validation for something good she could do for someone else.

Over the next few years some of my resident inmates were getting out of jail and going to work in flower shops on the outside. One inmate that I had for some time was Kara, who had been serving life for shooting her son over a drug deal. She came up for parole while she was in the flower program. She was a very hard core, tough woman, and smoked very heavily. Each member of her family had turned their backs on her. She was another beautiful designer, but still a bit rough around the edges.

I had a good florist friend who had partnered with me at the Expo '86 World's Fair in Vancouver. We decorated the Ontario and Alberta Pavilions and a V.I.P. lounge for the six month duration of the fair. He was a beautiful designer and had a lovely shop, however he was difficult to work for because he was so very fussy and you had to be good to work for him. He also smoked heavily and his staff turnover was very high. I once asked him if he would hire one of my designers. His answer was, "Hell no", but one day he called me and said, "Okay, June, do you have a good designer coming out?" His timing was great because Kara was being paroled. She was a great designer, reliable, and she smoked. I thought they were a match made in heaven, they could light each other's cigarettes! I called him back to tell him I had someone he should meet, and to give her a trial to see if her skills could fit his requirements. He did, they bonded really well, and worked together for years to come. Kara started a new life and her family forgave all her sad mistakes that happened while she was under the influence of drugs. Drug free, a good florist, and a whole new life; what more could anyone ask for?

Chapter Sixteen

Suzy, the young inmate that came into my floral program my very first day in the prison was the sad girl who came up to my design bench and remarked that she had never seen or smelled the fragrance of a fresh real rose. She was looking at the large floral vase full of red roses sitting in front of me. From that day forward all the time she spent in the floral program she enjoyed every minute that she could working with roses, her very favourite flower. Sadly, as time went by she was told she had a serious medical condition. She was coming close to completing her sentence and told me she really wanted to work in a flower shop upon her release. Finally the day arrived and Suzy was paroled but remained under close medical care with her illness, however she had a healthy outlook, felt pretty good, and went to work for another good florist friend of mine in the University of British Columbia area. She worked in their flower shop and they helped her find a place to live. They also got her to Alcoholics Anonymous and Narcotics Anonymous meetings because she had been a drug addict and needed the support to stay clean. She did stay clean and worked for them for some time, then moved on to a different store, but remained clean and working.

Some years went by and Suzy always stayed in touch. Sadly her terrible disease ended her life story, but over those years she was able to smell lots and lots of roses. When Suzy died, those that knew her also knew what the rose meant to her and each one placed a rose on her casket at her funeral. She deserved each and every one of them. From somewhere far beyond, Suzy watches over every rose garden that needs tender love and care. Every time over these many years, when I take a rose in my hand and put it up to my nose, I think of my friend Suzy.

Over the years right from day one with my first class every inmate that walked through door number seven became a beautiful floral designer. It was like when that door closed behind them and they entered the flower shop and the beauty and fragrance of all the flowers caught their attention something very special took place they were surrounded by one of nature's most beautiful commodities. As they worked with them and realized all the wonderful things they were capable of creating with flowers the magic started. It was those beautiful flowers that helped change each one of them. They appreciated and treasured every minute. The contentment and sense of pride, the beauty of nature helped to inspire them and fill a part of their lives that was missing "happiness". It's this that made them some of the best designers I've ever worked with and so proud of each one. You have to be happy and love what you do and do it with all your heart

Anita, a quiet older inmate that was so withdrawn and sad, had also changed. She was a good woman but her lover had left her, breaking her heart. This sent Anita to the edge and she shot him, a crime for which she received a life sentence of twenty-five years with no chance of parole for ten years. She was sorrowful for what she had done and served her time as a model inmate.

Anita became one of my best designers, winning the People's Choice Award with her arrangement, and she was able to design and make her daughter's wedding flowers while she was inside prison. All of her children married while she was serving her time, and when she was paroled she returned to her family. They loved her and always had been her support while she was incarcerated.

"Her Sad Eyes"

By June Strandberg

When I looked into her eyes
The life and twinkle was gone
Her days in prison were dark and long
It was like sadness was a shawl around her shoulders
The day would come and she could leave
But she would be much older
Could she be strong enough to start again
And for all the women in here lost and forgotten
Would she be able to stay sane
A special time came and she walked through door number seven
The beauty and fragrance that came from that room
Was going to change her life soon
I put that flower in her hand
I showed her if she came where she would stand
From that day forward she came every day
She had always been quiet with not a lot to say
Her shoulders were now straight
The sadness had left her and she knew then it wasn't too late
Those beautiful flowers were doing their magic once more
Her eyes twinkled and there was a smile on face
I knew I wanted to be there just in case
She needed kindness, encouragement and support
To put behind her the sad memory of last day in court
So with her beautiful floral designs
I have to say
She was able to help make sure

Someone else had a very happy day
For her it was about living and moving on
And for her that's the very day the sun shone

Chapter Seventeen

It was now 1995, my dear husband of twenty seven years, Bob succumbed to his cancer the previous year. His passing changed Casey's and my life. The three of us had worked together in the flower business for so long and we missed him very much. However we needed to keep busy and keep moving forward. During the last few years of Bob's life Casey and I had taken over the duties he was no longer able to handle. Moving put us closer to the prison and cut down on our traveling time. This worked better because some of our days were longer. A few years before his death we moved to a new home, a lovely apartment that overlooked the Fraser River at the New Westminster Quay. Bob was diagnosed with mouth cancer in 1984 and as his disease progressed he became less active, spending more time at home. His favourite activity, which he continued for as long as he could, was watching the boats and action on the river.

Even though we had gone through some sad days, Casey and I knew so well how important it was to keep a positive outlook. We couldn't take our troubles into the prison. We had taught the inmates to try to leave their upsets on the other side of door number seven, so it was up to us to do the same. Coming to work in the flower shop became a safe, beautiful sanctuary for them. It was up to Casey and I to maintain that and not let what was happening in our lives change the setting that had been created for them.

Coming to work at the prison most days could often be a challenge, but knowing we were always able to provide our inmates with the right message that their lives could still have happy moments. If they can let go of that desperate something that helped put them in prison. Try to appreciate and value what they have at this time and it will make their heart happier and lead them in the right direction. Happiness is a prize we give ourselves. The friends they've made within these grey walls. Family that waits for their return. Experience of working closely with nature. They can't focus on what's missing from their lives it's about being grateful for today.

Our job at the prison brought something different every day. Inmates came and went. Some left only to return for parole violations or another offence. Many people had the opinion that we should just lock them away and throw away the key. You needed to be in there every day, spend the time with them, listen to them, and above all, hear what they had to say. I was given a report of a study that had been done years prior by the Canadian federal government that showed that 85% of female offenders in Canada had been sexually, physically, or mentally abused. I think everyone deserves a second chance. Some of those lost women could be put on a new pathway. Some were lost, never able to find their way back ever again, so we did what we could with the power of our flowers to help heal their broken lives and it worked over and over again.

There were other alternative therapies in the prison that helped support the women to make positive changes in their lives. Each instructor gave one hundred percent when it came to helping the inmates in their programs, to make them realize that in time they could let go of the tragedies. That they could feel a sense of pride and trust in another human being and these programs let them know there were still people who believe in them. They were taught how to cook properly by the instructor in the prison kitchen, how to carefully sew in the tailor shop, or learn how to cut hair precisely in the hair dressing program. The ceramics program taught them the art of hand painting the individual pieces of clay and ceramics. There were arts and crafts programs that taught jewelry making, knitting, and crochet.

The prison chaplain was always there to help them through their sad days with wise words. The sweat lodge and healing circles helped the native inmates and there were meetings of Alcoholics Anonymous and Narcotics Anonymous held for anyone who was ready for change. The Salvation Army came in at Christmas to help make that time of year a little brighter with gifts and treats.

We were all there for the same reason and that was to let the inmates know the time would come when they would wake up to a perfectly beautiful day, look in a mirror, and get a glimpse of a face they loved to see. Without a doubt I believed we were working to make sure that day would come for every one of them.

Locked away on a top unit were the Doukhobor women. The Doukhobor's were a sect of religious extremists who protested many political issues by committing arson or displaying themselves nude in public. The BCCW had four of these inmates, and before long Beverly advised me that they would like to visit the flower shop. However, this would have to happen during a lunch break when all other inmates were in their units. The guards brought the women in a number of times and they enjoyed seeing the beautiful flowers and other items in the store. Sometimes they would submit a request to buy flowers to take back to their units.

It was important to make sure that there were no cigarette lighters or matches lying anywhere when these women came into the shop. In our first years in the prison the inmates were allowed to smoke in the prison, a privilege that eventually stopped. So it was that often one of my inmates would leave their cigarettes and lighter lying on their design bench during their breaks. Everyone knew that those little ladies liked to take matches or a lighter if they could. Shortly after our program began, the Doukhobors' were in the infirmary because they had been on a fast, became ill, and had to be on health watch. No one really knew how they managed to get matches or lighters, but they started a fire in the infirmary causing about $10,000 worth of damage. No one was hurt but their action caused a lot of smoke. This incident happened prior to permission being granted for them to visit the flower shop. I thought they were really sweet little women, they looked like anyone's grandmother, and the inmates also liked them. They were well spoken, kind, older women who had a belief system, and that's just how it was. Other than taking their clothes off, refusing to eat, and setting fires, they were a loveable group. However, I did keep a sharp eye when they paid us a visit. I wasn't keen on having a bonfire happening in the middle of the flower shop, but all-in-all we enjoyed having them visit us and it made them feel good to smell the flowers.

Then came the young boys from the Willingdon Youth Detention Centre. A group of their worst offenders were sent to BCCW temporarily and were sectioned off in D-Block, on the upper floor, across from B-Block. These young offenders also received permission to visit the flower shop during a lunch break since they were only moved in the prison when the women inmates were all locked in their units. They were escorted by their guard and liked the idea of being able to buy flowers for family and friends when they came to visit them. The first time they walked through the door I saw these good looking, clean shaven, tidy young men, with their snow-white t-shirts and sweats, who were very polite and well mannered. And they loved to buy flowers. I thought every one of them were really nice and I had a difficult time wrapping my mind around that any one of them had done something so bad that they were deemed dangerous. It was like someone had made a mistake, misjudged them, but I was wrong.

Beverly made sure we were aware of the kind of young men they were if we couldn't think that one of them ever contemplated doing something naughty. My experience with them was always pleasant and I hoped that one day they would all be on a road to a better life upon their release.

Chapter Eighteen

Wendy, a very pretty young woman with blond hair and lovely pale blue eyes, was doing time on a drug charge. Her husband had also done time, and they had two small children who were in foster care. One of the times they were both out on parole and staying in a rooming house in the infamous Vancouver downtown east side, they had been doing drugs when her husband fell out of the window on the second floor that left him paralyzed from the waist down, in a wheelchair, and needing constant care. He and Wendy had violated parole with their drug abuse and were sent back to prison. This was heart-breaking for Wendy. Having spent a lengthy time in prison, they had been labeled unfit parents. It was deemed unsafe for their kids to be with them, and soon she was told she was losing custody. To me this would have to be the very worst thing that could happen to her and even though she worked hard in the flower shop and was a good designer, she never kicked her drug habit as far as I know.

Wendy was ready for parole again four or five years later and before leaving the prison she came to see me and said I should make sure to see her if and when I was in her area. She told me I could find her at the corner of Gore and Hastings, which was a very seedy area of the city. She said she would have a white patio chair sitting at the corner. If she wasn't there when I went by she told me just to wait and she'd be right back. She said she wanted to see me for sure if I ever had the occasion to go that way, and mentioned I could wait in her chair.

Whenever Casey and I had the occasion to go downtown to deliver flowers to the hotels, we would often drive down Hastings Street. There were times, as we waited for traffic lights at Gore and Hastings, that sure enough there would be a couple of women standing on that corner who recognized us and would wave and call out a big, "Hello June and Casey!" They were always glad to see us. At least when we saw them we knew they were still alive, not in the safest place in town, but alive.

There were major changes happening at the prison in 2003. Beverly left for a new position elsewhere. Staff members were sad to see her leave and for sure the inmates were too. She was always there for them, a hands on program director who regularly walked the prison halls interacting with the inmates and giving them direction and support. She was the best advocate the women could have, and when she left that didn't happen ever again.

A new director took over who handled her job in a totally different manner. The first thing on her agenda was to move the flower shop out of the maximum security area to the open living unit in minimum security, where we stayed until the prison closed in 2004. Business continued as usual and I started training the women in minimum security to be florists, as well as returning to maximum security two days a week to continue to train inmates there, but in a different location than where our flower shop had been. It wasn't long after our move that there was talk of the prison closing, and on March 31, 2004, it was heart-breaking to walk out on the last day. Fourteen years behind those seven locked doors proved to be a life transforming experience, not just for me, but for my inmate students. The program did so much better than I ever dreamed it would.

During the turmoil of change in 2003 I received encouraging recognition for the work my program was achieving, giving incarcerated women inspiration and new hope for a better life, I was nominated for the YWCA Metro Vancouver Women of Distinction Award for Community Entrepreneurship. It was very exciting just to know I had been nominated, but then on the evening of June 5, 2003, Dean, Cindy, and Casey accompanied me to a prestigious awards dinner at The Westin Bayshore Hotel in downtown Vancouver. Luminaries from the Vancouver lower mainland business community, media outlets, and many public and private institutions, as well as the nominees from the numerous award categories gathered in the hotel ballroom to hear who the winners would be. It felt like the Academy Awards to me; I was excited at the prospect of winning and at the same time nervous that I might just be the winner among the six nominees in my category. A Royal Bank of Canada representative began her speech outlining the attributes of the winning nominee and I very soon realized she was talking about me! My name was announced as the winner and I was presented my award by Bramwell Tovey, Conductor of the Vancouver Symphony Orchestra, and the Royal Bank representative. Cameras flashed, recording this very special moment in my life, and then I gave my acceptance speech. The room was hushed as I spoke briefly about the experience of bringing a floral program to maximum security inmates and its success. As I ended my speech the room exploded in applause, I felt overwhelmed and so appreciated on that special night.

A little while after the award the federal government asked me to come out to the prison in the Fraser Valley to where some of my inmates had been transferred. Casey and I met with the Program Director to discuss bringing my floral training program there, however there were too many inconveniences and a very long daily drive, and we decided this new location was not suitable.

The turmoil in the prison during 2003 with the scandalizing story around the Pickton pig farm was causing a great deal of upset and unrest. It was during 2003 when the women all knew they were going to be moved. All to different locations depending on whether they were federal or provincial inmates. A lot of these women had been together for years and there were some strong friendships. They relied and supported each other through thick and thin, how would this affect them all.

Shortly before we closed our BCCW program the Pickton pig farm was already in the news. Dozens of marginalized women from the streets of Vancouver's dismal downtown east side began disappearing in the late 1990s, but not until the early years of the twenty-first century did authorities realize a serial killer was at work. DNA evidence of many of B.C.'s missing women was eventually found on the Coquitlam, B.C., pig farm and twenty-six murder charges were laid against the suspect. A police poster showing photographs of over fifty women missing in the province was publicly distributed, many of whom I recognized as having been prison inmates, and in particular eleven faces of women who had taken the floral program in BCCW. One I remember so well. She had served a major portion of her sentence, achieving a good level of effort towards gaining parole. The day she appeared before the parole board and was granted her release, she had dressed nicely and had her hair styled. She said good-bye to all of us and looked forward to being reunited with her baby girl and her other children. She was ready for a new life. She was never seen again.

I was also training a young inmate whose mother had been an inmate and whose name appeared on the missing women's list. Often times a mother and daughter were in prison at the same time. The inmates all knew each other so well, spending years, day after day, together. This horrific incident was very, very sad and difficult for all of them.

★★★

Reflections of a friend's life lost
No longer is she here.
Reminded that she paid the cost
A cost much too dear.

Those of us who loved her best
Remember how we tried
To help put her mind at rest.
But in failing this, she died.

Now her body is deceased
and her soul has learned to fly.
She has found in death; release
While we on earth; still cry.

★★★

UNTITLED POEM

As I walk the streets alone
thinking of things that are
unknown

People in alley ways are wasting
their life away

Will this be me, how much more
am I yet to see

An innocent mind next in line
the essence of time
Starts with crime, who's next?

★★★

THOSE WONDERFUL FLOWERS

by June Strandberg

I was born with two hands
And so lucky to always
Have flowers in them
With them came lots of love and beauty
To have lived all these years and love what I do
And know that it matters
What could be better
He's let me be the best
Because He made me lead designer
Over all the rest
So when that time does come
I'll be ready to go
And my design bench will be ready I know
How happy I am for all the year I've spent
And what every minute of every day has meant
But why does this bring tears to my eyes
They are tears filled with lots of love
Can you have happy tears run down your face
Oh! Yes you can
If I could catch them in a little glass
They would sparkle like diamonds
And they would be just as valuable

★★★

I WILL FIGHT

The look upon your face
Innocent you are
Sentenced for a deadly crime
The system's gone too far.

I will fight for freedom... in a positive way...
I will fight for you my people...'cause there is no other way.

We hold the key to the missing link...
"Taxpayers, I hereby sentence...you to think!"

Take a good look at the white man's lies...
"Oppressive Justice System"
Do you hear the Nation's cries?
The resistance continues...The Indigenous Are Strong,
We lived in the right...
White men lived in the wrong.

I will fight for my people...feather in my hand.
I will fight the unjust judgements...
The disease upon our land.
My Brothers...My Sisters
We must make our stand...
Together we will fight...
The truth is close at hand.

Chapter Nineteen

The seven doors were locked forever but on the other side another door opened for Casey and me and for any women who needed flowers in their lives, those special magical little gems that make life so much better. They cast their spell when you touch them and smelling the fragrance creates that warm feeling inside you, softening the sad times and helping to make the happy times happier. Being a florist is the very best thing I could have been.

In 2004 and a new chapter of my life began. I still had a piece of my dream left. There will always be women facing barriers, physical and mental challenges, as well as women who just need a change in their lives. I knew I was not finished yet. I needed to find a way to take Beginnings further. I had my 'outside' program tucked away in a safe place and I needed to look it over and see how to make it work.

I had just come through another challenge in my life. In 1996 I met Monty Strandberg, a very nice Danish gentleman. We were married in 1997 and had seven good years together. He was my third husband and also helped me with my flower business. He was very special to me, but in 2004 I again became a widow when he too died from cancer. I was alone once more and the prison was closing. I had two big voids in my heart. I knew I had come this far and, thinking of all the people who believed in me when sometimes I didn't believe in myself, for every person that crossed my path, that inspired my career, I realized there's nothing as real as a dream.

When the word started that BCCW would close, different organizations contacted me. One was the Elizabeth Fry Society, another The Wish Society. Several women's organizations asked if I would be interested in bringing my program to them. I met with some of them, laid out what I had in mind and what I thought would work, but for marginalized women and what my program had to offer, I found that I didn't feel comfortable with them. Each one was a wonderful society, but they had their own agenda and I didn't think I fit into it. I began to see how I could create my own non-profit society. Funding was the biggest challenge. Where would the support come from?

But a new opportunity arose when I met a very caring couple, Michael and Ann Wilson of the Phoenix Society. They were in the process of raising funds to build a residential treatment facility for recovering male drug addicts. After a lot of hard work their funding was in place and their building was nearing completion.

As soon as Casey and I met Michael and Ann I knew we were on the same page. They wanted a better life for men with addictions, and I wanted marginalized women to have better opportunities, so in 2006 my partnership with the Phoenix Centre began.

We opened Just Beginnings, a non-profit society with a flower shop, coffee house, and a registered floral training centre. I formed a board of directors and the first person I asked to be on my board was the woman who had the biggest heart in the world and always believed in what I had done. Beverly Roest became chairwoman of the board, and who better could I get? From the day she walked through the doors of Just Beginnings and until the very last, her wisdom and strength kept us going, even through our struggles.

My purpose was to train marginalized women, some who were just coming from prison, recovering addicts, and women that had suffered abuse.

We also had a group of great women who wanted a change in their career, one that had been at the bank too long, and another who just wanted a break from her government job. These women were a great influence on our marginalized ladies, and they all mixed together very well. Lots of good friendships blossomed in each class through understanding each other's life experiences and respecting one another, all together creating beautiful designs with flowers and all feeling a sense of pride when they had completed the course. Sharing their ideas with one another, it was important for them not only to learn to be florists together but to enjoy each other's company even though they all came from different walks of life.

It was a slow start, but soon people got to know where we were and even some of our customers from the prison used us for their flower needs. Our wedding business started to build and our coffee counter in the corner of our flower shop attracted people who worked at Surrey Memorial Hospital, and the medical buildings close by, as well as the employees of Phoenix. Some of the men who lived in the residence also supported the flower shop.

Our biggest corporate funder was Vancity Credit Union, who gave us our start and helped over the next four years. Coast Capital Savings was another contributor; we received great support from these two financial institutions. I also had a great deal of support from my board, and Michael Wilson always had wise words of advice when I needed it. My niece Michelle volunteered her time to help me, not only in my office, but also by assisting me in the classroom. Beverly Roest was always there with support, advice, and much volunteer effort. Her husband Jack worked tirelessly to promote our floral trade school, making contact with government offices and other organizations that could use our services.

The Surrey Pre-Trial Services Centre, a provincial jail operated by the British Columbia government, held an annual job fair
to assist inmates find employment upon their release. Non-profit
societies such as the Inner City Women's Initiatives Society and
Options Community Services Society attended to help provide
many other types of support needed to help released offenders get
on the right track. The first time that Jack Roest and I attended
this event, I recognized a familiar face as the doors opened to
allow the first group of inmate's access to the fair. It was Frances,
an inmate I had lost contact with several years before the prison
closed. She came to me, her eyes filled with tears, and I gave her a
big hug. She was much thinner and walked with a limp, the result
of being shot in the hip. She said she was coming up for parole and
asked if she could come to work for us. I told her to come and
see me the minute she got settled, and yes I would hire her. Sadly,
when Frances called to say she was coming into the shop, she did
not arrive and that was the last I heard from her.

Over my years working with so many women marginalized by
society because of their lifestyles, crimes, and time served in prison,
I had tried but failed to maintain contact with some of them. I
realized after all this time I needed to be grateful for all the great
things that have happened, to ride above the disappointment of
not being able to follow through with women such as Frances; to
be there to make sure they were going to make it. I cherish every
minute I have had with every student that crossed my path, no
matter what walk of life they came from. My connections with
them have always led me in the right direction. I've had so many
reasons to smile and so many roses to share, and to know in my
heart I did my best and did it my way.

Each class I had at Just Beginnings was special. Every student
gave their all, and it was a pleasure to teach them. Some started
their own flower business, others went on to work at flower shops,
or at floral wholesalers. Collectively all my students from Just
Beginnings were lovely designers.

During the time at Just Beginnings we also trained women with physical and mental disabilities. Some were a little more challenging than others, but without a doubt each and every one of them was influenced by the flowers. As I trained them, they took direction very well. They were always gentle with the flowers, and being able to work with them and actually create something beautiful gave them such a gift. The sweet, simple, beautiful flowers were the magic something that touched each one of them, inspired them, and helped give them the confidence to realize there was something special they were able to do. One of these students was able to start a small flower business with the full support of her family. A resource centre specializing in clients with disabilities was a great support to her and encouraged her to set up her flower business right at their centre. She has done very well, even going to the auction and floral wholesaler for her supplies.

Chapter Twenty

In late summer of 2008, The Vancouver Organizing Committee (VANOC) for the 2010 Winter Olympics put out a call for florists regarding the victory bouquets for the medal winning athletes. The meeting was attended by Penny Handford, one of my very hard working volunteer board members, who was very active in promoting Just Beginnings, and responsible for writing all our funding proposals. She told me approximately 58 were there, most of them younger florists. VANOC said it would be best if florists paired up to do the job. Penny found that most of the young florists were talking amongst themselves, but there was a much older lady standing alone who didn't seem to be included in any of the conversations. Penny struck up a conversation with her and told her she was representing Just Beginnings and maybe it would be a good idea for her to have a talk with me if she was interested in pursuing the Olympic contract.

The florist was Margitta Schulz, owner of Margitta's Flower Boutique at North Vancouver's Lonsdale Quay. Penny set up a conference call with herself, Margitta, her business manager Patricia, and myself. I had never heard of Margitta. There were not many florists in the Lower Mainland that I didn't know, so just before our conference call I phoned my good friend Carol at one of the wholesale companies and asked her if she knew Margitta and could she tell me a bit about her. Carol said, "You'll really like her, June. She's a very nice lady and an older florist like you." I took that as a compliment, I think.

So the evening of our call, Penny and I were in the Just Beginnings flower shop and Margitta and her business partner were at their flower shop. The call started and Penny said, "June, how about you go first and introduce yourself." I said, "Hi, Margitta. I'm June Strandberg and I've been a florist for sixty-two years." On the other end of the phone Margitta answered, "Holy Shit". That's the moment I knew without a shadow of doubt she was the florist I wanted to go to the Olympics with. I thought for someone who had never met me she had a lot of guts to answer that way. When Margitta made that statement, Penny and I were shocked! We talked some more and agreed to meet. Our meeting went well and we agreed on how our proposal would be handled.

Because I had provided floral work for the Expo '86 World's Fair, I knew what it took to take on a big contract. I also had done so much piece work in my prison program that I knew how long it took to make single pieces and worked out how many bouquets a designer could make in one hour to know I needed twenty-three students to make the required 1,800 Olympic bouquets.

All proposals were to be submitted to VANOC by the deadline at the end of September 2008. The proposal had to clearly show what your florist experience was, how and where the work would be done, as well as cost estimates for wages and all supplies, deliveries, packaging, and incidentals. VANOC set down the budget for each victory bouquet.

In early November the proposals were short listed to three teams; Margitta's and Just Beginnings were one of them, and we were so pleased to be in that final group. The first week of December came along with a wonderful email telling us we had been awarded the Olympic contract.

We had a first meeting with VANOC to get the information we needed to make the bouquets. I met Margitta in the main lobby of the VANOC building. She was just recovering from a knee operation, and I had an arthritic knee. She had a walking cane and we were both limping. I said to her, "We'd better try not to limp when we go upstairs. Do you think they'll know how old we are?" Margitta was going to be sixty-five, and I was seventy-six. "If they know they might wonder if we will make it to the Olympics!"

She answered, "I'll leave my cane here," and away we went doing our best not to limp and stand as straight as we could. We did it, and we were great!

Over the weeks we presented VANOC with twenty three different styles for the victory bouquet. Margitta and I worked on these together knowing that everything in them had to be from British Columbia. Remembering it was winter time, most of the flowers would be coming from greenhouses. Finally we knew we wanted the bouquets to be the colours of the Olympics; green and blue. The foliage leaves and grasses that we chose did grow outside in B.C during the summer months. We knew we had to have a strong supply of everything for 1,800 bouquets, and they had to look and be durable. We chose green spider mums, hypericum berries framed in large green leaves, ferns, and grass, then tied it together with the blue Olympic ribbon. The bouquets had to be safe and have no sharp parts and no strong scents from the flowers because of the possibilities of allergic reaction. We received a lot of kudos for our bouquets.

Chapter Twenty-One

Earlier in 2008 I had told my students we were bidding on the contract and how much I wanted to do this because it meant they could all be part of this wonderful opportunity, and together we could accomplish this. So with this wonderful news, our work began. From the list of past students I wanted on my team were ones that had gone on to jobs in flower shops. This project was a commitment for each participant and they would need time off from their jobs during the Olympics to make the bouquets. Every employer was excited for them to be involved, and fully supported them in coming back to work with me and be a part of the excitement.

Our twenty-three wonderful designers had such varied backgrounds. Some were changing careers, while others suffered from physical or mental handicaps. Some were returning from military duty in Afghanistan and suffered from post-traumatic stress disorder. Many with significant health issues, some were battered women, and others were recovering drug addicts, sex trade workers, or women paroled from jail. We also had women who were immigrants or refugees with little skill in English. Together they were a team of women to be proud of. Making the Olympic bouquets meant something different to each one of them, but collectively it was being as close to the podium as they could be. Every morning when they came in to do their shift they knew they had helped make those wonderful Olympic bouquets they saw on television the night before.

We started each morning playing the song "Hallelujah" sung by K.D. Lang at the opening ceremonies of the 2010 Winter Olympics, and ended each day with our Winter Olympics theme song, "I Believe". The words were fitting, as if the songs were written for my designers as well.

I believe in the power of you and I
Stand tall and make the world proud
Stand tall for what's right

One week before our starting date I had all twenty-three designers come in together. Margitta and I had everything ready for them to make one Olympic bouquet each. Each woman took her place at tables, then Margitta and I demonstrated the bouquet, with the others following us. Each designer got it the first time around!

When we had completed the bouquets we tied them off with the Olympic blue ribbon, then held them high above our heads and I said, "You did it, we did it together, we're ready!" There were several media groups there that day, and they were impressed with what had just taken place.

On the first day of starting to design the Olympic bouquets, while the students were all working together, my designer in the flower shop called me to say that there was someone to see me. I went upstairs and, to my surprise, Brandie was standing there. I knew she had been paroled and was living somewhere in Surrey, but I hardly recognized her. She was extremely thin, very pale, and had very little hair on her head. Brandie gave me a big hug and said she knew I was going to be making the Olympic bouquets and she wanted to come and help out. She also wondered if I could give her work. Brandie told me she had cancer and was undergoing treatments across the street at the Surrey Memorial Hospital, and felt she had beaten the disease. I said when she had finished her treatments, and felt better, to phone me. Brandie was happy that I would let her come to work and, after a short visit with her that day, she mentioned she had married an inmate from another Pacific Regional Correctional Centre who had also been paroled. That was the last time I saw her. Within weeks of coming into the store Brandie's then husband had stabbed her to death. Such a tragic end to a very sad, wasted life.

We assembled bouquets every day, two days ahead of when they would be needed. Safeway supplied us with cardboard, biodegradable, recyclable banana boxes to pack all the bouquets in. Each bouquet had a little biodegradable bag filled with some water tied to the bottom of each bouquet to keep them fresh, as all bouquets had to be delivered one day in advance to every Olympic venue throughout the Vancouver, Richmond, North Vancouver, and Whistler areas on a set schedule.

Every Friday the young woman in charge of making sure everything went like clockwork with the flowers called me to say, "June your flowers arrived in perfect condition and right on time. Each bouquet was perfect; not one damaged petal." I told my designers how proud we were of them all. At the end of the games, VANOC sent us a wonderful letter saying we had done a phenomenal job.

When the Olympic athletes raise their bouquets above them, they are holding high the beautiful work of all my women that had won painful victories against daunting odds. Just as athletes obtain their very best by training hard and pushing their limits, my Olympic florists achieved their personal best by believing in themselves and stepping forward with dignity and self-confidence. They don't award medals for the victories of kicking your drug habit, serving prison time, not turning another trick, or recovering from years of sexual abuse. The only award for this is jail time, and you can lose your very soul. The only time you would get attention from the media was if your face appeared on the list of the Missing and Forgotten Women of British Columbia, but by then it was too late.

The Olympic contract ended and it was time to retire after sixty-two years and reaching the age of seventy-six. When I walk down memory lane my thoughts go back to all the women I have taught over the years. What those beautiful flowers did for my life, and how they inspired me and led me down a path that let me teach each and every one of them the power of flowers. Flowers let them know how much they had accomplished and felt something they never thought possible, a touch of pride in what they could do and how it feels. That's all that matters.

I am very grateful for my success as a florist (thanks Uncle Tom), and that I was led in the right direction and be able to share my knowledge with others. The good times and all the laughs I've treasured with best friends and designing buddies for nearly forty years are priceless. Carol and Dale always shared their knowledge whenever they could, many of my students have stayed in touch with me on Facebook, and sometimes with a phone call, a card, or a dinner together. They are all precious memories, and I feel so happy knowing my floral program worked.

What a magnificent journey I've had. All the wonderful women I met created the very best rose garden I could have walked through. Every one of them was there with me. Life has a way of giving people second chances, so that's why it's important to keep trying.

To all my women behind those Seven Locked Doors, and also to ones on this side, I will always cherish our connection. To know in my heart those magical flowers helped them love what they were doing and realize as individuals that they mattered, mattered so very much.

Introductory Book On Floral Design

The Art of Floral Design by Norah T. Hunter
One of the best books on the basics of floral design. I used this
book in my schools over the years. It is a book that introduces
you to the complete elements and principals of design.

Floral Design Magazine
Includes design principals. This is a very special,
excellent and inspirational magazine.
Subscriptions by mail are available from:
Floral Design Magazine, 17 Hill Street, Paeroa, New Zealand 3600
On line contact information:
www.floralartmall.com
email: info@floralartmall.com

This version is the final with corrections approved by June, March 31.

For Kathleen Bizjak

For investing all her valuable time in helping me process my book and transferring it into a Word document. I appreciated her sincere interest and intrigue in the subject of my story. Thank you, Kathleen, for all your support and kindness.

Printed in Canada